THE POETRY OF POSTWAR JAPAN

IOWA TRANSLATIONS

Contemporary Korean Poetry
Modern Chinese Poetry
Mihail Eminescu
The Poetry of Postwar Japan

GENERAL EDITORS

Paul Engle
Hualing Nieh Engle

THE POETRY OF
POSTWAR JAPAN

Edited by
KIJIMA HAJIME

UNIVERSITY OF IOWA PRESS
IOWA CITY

The Collegiate Associations Council of The University of Iowa
contributed funds toward the production of this book.

Library of Congress Cataloging in Publication Data
Main entry under title:

The Poetry of postwar Japan.

   (Iowa translations)
   Includes bibliographical references and index.
   1.   Japanese poetry—20th century—Translations into
English.   2.   English poetry—Translations from Japanese.
I.   Kijima, Hajime, 1928–   II.   Series.
PL782.E3P6   895.6'1'508   75–17718
ISBN 0–87745–055–2

University of Iowa Press, Iowa City 52242
© 1975 by The University of Iowa. All rights reserved
Printed in the United States of America

FOREWORD

Theology once believed that "translation" could mean direct removal to heaven of the body without intervening death. All too often in being translated, the poem loses its life.

Literal translation of a poem into bare prose may help understanding, but the plain text of a literal version may not be accurate to the poem, for what a poet writes is not a literal account of his life, but an imaginative vision of it. Only a translator with imagination can truly translate the imaginative language of a poem.

The Iowa Translation Series brings together people of creative talent with those expert in a language. We believe that in the hazardous twentieth century men of good mind and good will must talk to each other or die. We believe that poetry is the highest form of talk, and that translating it is therefore an honor and a privilege, as well as one of the toughest jobs known to man.

The tone of postwar Japanese poetry is dramatized when Yoshimasu Gozo says that when he shouts the first line of his poem, "A carving knife stands up madly in the morning." The human voice has such power, and especially at its highest level in poetry. When Tanikawa Shuntaro writes about a woman that "within her someone is wounded," he is speaking for the reckless time in which

• v

we all try to survive. When Kijima Hajime writes, "Without red, I can never have a color," he is really saying that without suffering, fire, blood, intensity, he has no life and there is no Japan. When Tamura Ryuichi writes, "A bird falls, so there is height," he is imaginatively reassuring us that life not only measures the physical world, but that even in its falling it asserts life. When he says that "I could not dilute the words with meanings like whiskey with water," he is offering the primal push of human experience, deeper than literature. Postwar poetry, without denying the ancient and beautiful traditions, seems determined to penetrate the daily life of its cities for the daily power of its images. The concrete of Japan's buildings is matched by the concrete language of its poetry.

It is the duty of translation to recreate (not imitate) the original poem, which is itself a recreation of the original idea-emotion which startled the poem out of the writer's mind and into language. In the case of Japan, the shock of war seems to have shaped these poems into the shock of language. Words snarl, vivify, slash, cut, draw blood. The translators have had the tough job of making English words try to do the same. It is an act which will be forever defeated, and must be forever attempted.

Japanese poetry in English will, we hope, prove that verse has been one of that country's great productions since 1945.

Paul Engle and *Hualing Nieh Engle*
Directors, International Writing Program
School of Letters, The University of Iowa

ACKNOWLEDGMENTS

Editor's Acknowledgments
Kijima Hajime

I would like to thank the translators who permitted me to include their work in this anthology.

And also I would like to thank Oda Kyuro, the president of the publishing house Shichosha in Tokyo, who gave me permission to make a copy of manuscripts in preparation. From these manuscripts I was able to form a part of this anthology. He expects to publish an anthology of modern Japanese poetry in Japan.

And I must express my gratitude to Paul and Hualing Engle, whose persistent will for international communication encouraged me most; to Andrea Miller in the Asia Society, whose wide knowledge of this type of literary activity in the United States gave me the perspective for completion; and to Sharon Rohner, who typed the manuscripts quickly and exactly.

But above all, my special thanks go to John Bean, former assistant for the International Writing Program, who gave me useful and friendly advice constantly as a poet. Even where his name does not appear, he made the translations better and finer, giving the translators his useful suggestions.

Also assisting with individual final versions of individual poems were the following: John Batki, Onuma Tadayoshi, Larry Levis, and Arvind Krishna Mehrotra.

General Editors' Acknowledgments

Paul Engle
Hualing Nieh Engle

Special acknowledgment is made to the Louis W. and Maud Hill Family Foundation of Saint Paul, Minnesota (A. A. Heckman, former executive director, John D. Taylor, present executive director) now known as the Northwest Area Foundation. After years of helping the Program in Creative Writing with funds which went to young American writers, some of whom later won the Pulitzer Prize, the National Book Award, or the Yale Series of Younger Poets, the Foundation began aid to the International Writing Program. This helped bring established and widely published writers from all parts of the world. A major grant was given for translation, making possible a large increase in the number of books to appear in the Iowa Translations Series.

Grotto Foundation, Inc., also of Saint Paul (Louis W. Hill, Jr., president, A. A. Heckman, secretary) has helped the International Writing Program each year bring a distinguished writer from Japan. A. A. Heckman is probably one of the most innovative Foundation heads in this country: under his direction, three Foundations (the Hill Family, Grotto, and Avon, now named Jerome) have supported creative writing not only by American talent, but by writers from such distant places as Nigeria, Japan, Greece, Indonesia, Brazil, and from many other countries. We doubt that any

Foundation officer ever helped literature in so many languages. The editor of this anthology, Kijima Hajime, was able to join the International Writing Program and work on this anthology because of assistance from the Grotto Foundation.

It seems to us remarkable that three Foundations in the Upper Midwest should have such an imaginative view of the human world. Why? The Hill family has always had a special interest in Japan, as well as in the cultural life of its own area. James J. Hill was a strong promoter of Japanese-American relationships. Louis W. Hill, Sr., founder of the Hill Family Foundation, had a deep concern for Japan, its culture as well as its trade. His son, the present Chairman of the Board of the Hill Family Foundation, has visited Japan many times and has been host to Japanese delegations in the Twin Cities.

Help from these Foundations has been spiritual as well as financial. By proving that they had faith in our projects, they gave us faith. The books already published are from the Chinese, Korean, and Romanian, and books are expected from Hungarian, Russian, the three major languages of Yugoslavia, the fifteen major languages of India, Polish, Dutch, more from the Chinese, and others, and are evidence of work as well as of faith.

Additional contributions have come from John Deere Co., Moline; Northern Natural Gas, Omaha; Meredith Publishing Co., Des Moines; Maytag Co., Newton; Ford Foundation, New York; *Des Moines Register*; Department of State, Washington; Jurzykowski Foundation, New York; Kosciuszko Foundation, New York; American Republic Insurance Co., Des Moines; Cowles Charitable Trust, New York; First National Bank, Iowa City; Iowa State Bank and Trust Co., Iowa City; International Telephone and Telegraph, New York; Iowa Manufacturing Co., Cedar Rapids; Mr. and Mrs. William R. Shuttleworth, Cedar Rapids; Amana Refrigeration, Amana; The Asia Foundation, San Francisco; Book-of-the-Month Club, New York; Mrs. Marshall Field; The Hon. W. Averell Harriman; The Johnson Foundation, Racine; The Overbrook Foundation, New York; Tension Envelope Corp., Kansas City; and others. They also give because they believe.

All of our efforts would be impossible without the support of The University of Iowa, long a zealous patron of all the arts: Willard L. Boyd, president, Duane Spriestersbach, dean of the Graduate College, Dewey Stuit, dean of the College of Liberal Arts, John C. Gerber, director of the School of Letters, Darrell Wyrick, director of The University of Iowa Foundation. While other universities suspected the imagination, they supported it.

John Richardson, Jr., assistant secretary of state for Educational and Cultural Affairs, has been constantly helpful. Frank Tenney of the Department of State, and Conrad Stolzenbach, Jr., of the American Embassy, Tokyo, were especially helpful with Japan.

The Japan Foundation, Tokyo, enabled us to confer with Kijima Hajime and other poets included in this book while we visited Tokyo.

ON POSTWAR JAPANESE POETRY

Kijima Hajime

Postwar Japanese poetry emerged from the ashes. During the wartime, the poets who were not influenced by the ultra-nationalistic military activities were rare, and almost all poets were mobilized to write war-encouraging poems. Spontaneously, rather than by being forced, they participated in this kind of literary effort. And of course, no literary works of endurance could come of such activities. As a result, when Japan was defeated by the Allied Forces in 1945, there was no base upon which the new poets could stand—only the so-called "Given Democracy."

Ashes, vacuum, and "Given Democracy." But nothing creative can be expected from these.

The writers who had been ardent militarists yesterday suddenly became "democrats." Their guilty consciences caused them to accuse the then famous poets of their fascistic literary activities during the wartime. Thus began the long controversy about the responsibility of the poets during the war. Critics pointed out the relation between the ultra-nationalistic totalitarianism and the traditional psyche which was represented frantically in the war poems. Could such a relation be found and analyzed well enough? Hot debates continued.

In 1946 a serious article was published by Professor Kuwabara about the traditional short poem, *haiku*. I want to quote the concise summary of this article and its result as presented by Professor Keene:

It is easy for a Japanese, even of modest education, to write a poem in seventeen or thirty-one syllables. An ability to dash off a *haiku* at a drinking party is prized as a social asset. Naturally enough, the quality of most amateur *haiku* is deplorable. However, the most influential article written about the *haiku* since the war (in 1946), "On Second Class Art" ("Daini Geijutsu-ron") by Kuwabara Takeo, a professor of French literature at Kyoto University, asserted that the difference between a *haiku* composed by an acknowledged master and one by a bank clerk or a railway engineer was hardly perceptible. Taking a hint from the method used by I. A. Richards in *Practical Criticism*, he asked a group of colleagues to evaluate various *haiku*, some by masters and some by dubs, first removing the names of the poets. The results were so chaotic that Kuwabara felt justified in his claim that most people judge *haiku* by the poet's reputation and not by the works themselves. He asked if it were likely that a short story or a long poem by a master would be confused with one by an amateur, and concluded that the *haiku* must be a second class art, not objectionable as a mildly artistic diversion for amateurs, but certainly not to be considered a serious vehicle of literature.

Kuwabara's article aroused enormous controversy, as was to be expected, and diverted many budding young *haiku* poets to other fields. It is difficult to say that an art with the enormous following of *haiku* is not flourishing, but Kuwabara's article certainly shook the foundations of the art in a manner from which it has not recovered. The *tanka*, though not specifically a target of Kuwabara's, was susceptible to much the same criticism. It moreover has suffered from its intimate association, as the oldest and therefore "purest" Japanese verse form, with the ultra-nationalistic activities during the war. The *tanka* poets were vociferous in the adulation they offered to the mystique of the Imperial Family and the Japanese civilizing mission. The student who today writes *tanka* is therefore regarded with suspicion as a possible embryonic fascist, no matter what subject he may choose. The seventeen-year-old boy who assassinated the leader of the Socialist Party wrote a *tanka* in his prison cell before committing suicide. (Donald Keene, *Modern Japanese Poetry* [University of Michigan, 1964].)

One thing I wish to add is the fact that *tanka* became the form of death poema by soldiers and generals who were executed as war criminals after World War II. Almost all made death poems as an accompaniment of their rigid rituals. But they never composed *haiku* when they were about to die. Thus, for the relation of the war to traditional poetry, *tanka* was actually more deeply involved than *haiku*, as Professor Keene has pointed out. And after the devastating war, many poets were forced to become keenly aware of the sentimental lyricism in *tanka*. What elements in the Japanese psyche could mold themselves into ultra-nationalistic militarism? Poets could not avoid this question. Modernity in Japan itself did mean the imitation of Western expansionistic civilization, which was the stepfather of militaristic provocative activities by Japan—or was it not? Reflections like these kept coming.

Fundamentally, in modern Japanese lyricism there must have been something fragile that tended to be sentimentally totalitarian, and poets should have criticized this element, but actually they promoted this tendency without being aware of it.

The ultra-nationalistic power oppressed all literary activities: modern, avant-garde, and proletarian. But after the surrender of resistants to this oppression, people who were educated militaristically became rather more and more enthusiastic about the governing class's ultra-nationalism. So, oppressed by power, and surrounded by the warmongering people, many poets could not write their own personal feelings even clandestinely, or even inside their own hearts.

But the unknown poets or the poets-to-be were mumbling, and chewing over the whole experience, and not a few genuine poets died during the war. Kusuda Ichiro was one of them. He wrote the following lines before he was killed on some battlefield.

Where this wind blows itself out
The hollows of valleys
Without air or clouds

The cries of beasts nibbling
At the thistle's stinging leaves,
All rush up into a blank sky
Like violent soldiers.
Humans are being killed,
Being killed.
Look at this tree,
Listen to this stone.
Inside the cracks of the earth
Many lives continue.

Various blood billows up
And gleams in daylight
Like the coolies' greased foreheads.
. . . .
Evening was stained and looted
This eye witnessed the devastation
. . . .
They were excluded from sleep
They slept standing, like trees

(from "Dark Songs," translated by Kijima Hajime)

In these lines the young poet was keenly aware of what the war was bringing about.

He can be called a forerunner of the postwar poets. And this poem was published after the war by his friend Ayukawa Nobuo, who became one of the most influential poets and critics, founding the poetry group Arechi (The Waste Land) in 1947. As is clearly shown by its name, this poetry group Arechi started its literary activities under the influence of T. S. Eliot, considering this age of ours as that of devastation, futility, and despair.

It must be added that this forming of the poetry group Arechi was made during wartime, not officially, but with some of the same feeling, coming spontaneously in separate places, that "hope is abominable for us, and despair is more suitable for us in 1941 and

1942" (Ayukawa Nobuo, *The Wartime Diary*). There was no vacuum for them. They were breathing the new poetic air through destruction.

What should not be forgotten is that already in the nineteen twenties and thirties all the trends of modern or post-modern poetry had been introduced into Japan. After 1868 when feudalism ended, within the next forty to sixty years, Japanese poetry changed its dress several times—romanticism, naturalism, symbolism, dadaism, futurism, surrealism, intellectualism, proletarianism—and stood as a contemporary with Western poetry having the same kind of consciousness in common. However, it did not find any tie with Oriental poetry at all, even in the field of folklore or popular lyrics. It faced toward the West always, this tendency still continues, and nobody can foresee the prospect of change. Perhaps this comes from the linguistic and political isolation of Japan, and also from her unprecedented modernization in Asia. But Japanese poets have tended to feel a strong affinity with the West, and in the last stage before World War II they felt the same artistic consciousness as the Western avant-gardists. For example, Takiguchi Shuzo, who was once put into prison and became one of the most respected art critics after the war, was a colleague of those international surrealists like André Breton and Paul Eluard. The reason why the police had arrested surrealists was simple. The men in power thought surrealism not understandable, and therefore dangerous for them. Even though Takiguchi stopped writing poetry very early, his would be considered as one of the forerunners of postwar poetry, and under his influence not a few young poets began to concentrate their energy upon the imaginative. Here is an example of his poetry.

Virgin decorations
Ashes of innumerable inverted candles
Branches and flowers of transparent trees

Roars of infinite mirrors and
Spasms of windows of houses

My whole body
In the water fossil increasing its brightness day by day

My desire swims none the less
I am the noble bastard of the huge chandelier called azure

No one calls me the sphinx of love

My dream, in the fable of jasper,
Glitters all the more blue

("The Desire of the Fish," translated by Sato Hiroaki)

The poet who criticized the rising ultra-nationalistic tendencies most severely before the war was Oguma Hideo. He died in 1940, and was the last major proletarian poet who resisted very strongly the inclination toward fascism until his death. He expressed himself openly, and criticized his fellow poets and novelists bitterly but humorously after the regime forced the proletarian writers union to disband. He tried to write more colloquially than others.

Even if darkness
Blinds the earth forever
Our rights will always
Awaken.
Roses appear
Black in the darkness,
But if sunlight strikes them
Their color burns.

Grief and sorrow are our share,
Not theirs,
But they can have

Neither joy nor laughter.
I know all about darkness.
Therefore I believe light is coming.
Comprehend the hard meaning,
Comrades,
Of our search for fire:
We even strike our fists on stones.

Millions of voices
Cry in the dark.
The air is trembling and it illuminates
The windows.
It feels its way as a key does
And it brings light,
And it brings victory.

Never be useless and silent
When you are near roses.
Surely action
Is the synonym of hope.
Surely your emotion is a brilliant bridegroom.

So get ready.
Your carriage is coming.
You are going to welcome your bride.
You'd better get started.
Blow your horn's thunder,
Whip the horses along,
And make the clear sound
Of your loud wheel-track song.

("Starting Song of Our Carriage," translated by Kijima Hajime)

When the poetry group Retto (Archipelago) was formed in 1958, it intended to follow and develop this line of Oguma's with much more imaginative experimentation, like that of Takiguchi's.

Between these two main poetry groups, Arechi and Retto, there was one common awareness—the rumination over war experience. Of course, among those poets who did not belong to these two groups, the same feeling existed. How to reorganize the images, sounds, and deep feelings of wartime was the main concern of many poets. In the totalitarian war where almost all Japanese people were involved, nobody could avoid the disastrous results, mental and physical. So the naming of "Postwar Poetry" was irresistible and quite usable, until the generation with no experience and memory of war began to appear.

Every nation has its own memorable dates. Every person, too. Independence, confusion, and revolution. Love, crisis, and self-discovery. For postwar Japanese poetry the special date was 1945, because a new poetry began to emerge. But the date does not mean simply the defeat of militarism and the birth of a new nation. It also indicates a tremendously unfathomable image-burden for us. August 6th. Who can cope with the first event in the whole history of mankind with his imagination?

Together with the helplessness of soldiers, this unprecedented image of actual genocide haunted the postwar poets. *The Inferno* of the present age should have been written in Japanese. Perhaps no overwhelming poem has been written yet about the whole human experience of World War II. Let us read a memorable poem written by Ando Tsuguo who was born in 1919.

"On August 6th, 1945 at 8:15 a.m.
the first atomic bomb in human
history, dropped on Hiroshima,
branded on the granite a human
shadow sitting eternally at rest."

Rosy crystallized sunlight creeps around.
Now over the earth
The damp mold covering the lower world
Widens.

It increases a billion times faster
Than human activity.
It has been a long time
Since we wished to exterminate
That castrated shadow;
Since that day we stopped
Walking on two legs.

But we refuse to walk
On four legs forever—
Since our legs and arms have grown
To unmatching sizes.
With our hands placed forward obsequiously
On the earth,
We crawl around gladly
On our knees.

Since we saw the immense mushroom cloud
A dark purple that day
In the rosy crystallized sky,
Our bellies swelled up
Like those of pregnant women,
And from our navels an oil
Trickles continually.

How fussy we are about its amount—
Increasing? No.
We quarrel with each other about soiling
What was just cleaned.
How we laugh at these pointless arguments
With groans
As if our lungs were translucent.
We have no need now
To hide our genitals,
Nor enough time to bother with them.
All this pain is caused
By one problem: how to get rid

Of this dark red, swollen,
Unmanageable navel.
On the navel eyes grow,
And a nose,
And on the bald head
We check for downy hair quivering
Like dry rice in a field;
Turning the navel
Over again and again for a close inspection
Is the most solemn duty
In our daily schedule.
And therefore we crawl out gladly
Into the rosy crystallized sunlight
On our knees.

A long time has passed
Since we began
To extinguish our widening shadows
Over the earth.

A long time has passed
Since we began to forget
The dark home country
From which we'd started.

("The Book of the Dead," translated by Kijima Hajime)

Thus the abnormal mental condition resulting from the war continued. The wounded, the mutilated, and the ghosts were rampant in postwar Japanese society, even though people were taught about democratic reconstruction. How can they disappear in the imagery of sensitive poets?

During this time, curiously enough, or rather naturally enough, the healthy appeared singular and prominent. When Tanikawa Shuntaro began to publish his poems which had no war shadows, his works were thought to be fresh and clear, and attracted attention. But, although he was considered to be totally free from the influence of the war, it was not true. Such an interpretation is superficial.

About Tanikawa's formative years, let us hear the opinion of Iwata Hiroshi who belongs to the same generation:

> Then [during the war—Kijima] the junior high school students, who were too young to be desperately intoxicated with the war cause, but too mature to overlook the war reality, were opening their keen adolescent eyes in the vague freedom that was allowed only for noncombatants. In an over-strained period, to be wise one must always be on the alert, and also be abnormally sensitive. Day and night the junior high school students at that time used much sharper and purer imaginations than those who spent their adolescence in the other periods.

This remark of Iwata's about their adolescence can be applied to Tanikawa Shuntaro and other poets of the same age. And when the new poetic generation gathered together, forming a group named Kai (Oars) in 1953, it was thought that a third group besides Arechi and Retto was appearing. But actually the members of this group, too, were very concerned about the war and its results. The works of the poetess Ibaragi Noriko, one of the founders of this group, show that quite clearly.

So it can be said that paradoxically enough all the intense experiences of the war absurdly nurtured and prepared the important and distinctive voices in postwar poetry. In a sense, its intensity guaranteed the artistic quality of the poetry as long as it lasted in the poets' minds and among the public.

Thus the critical moment for postwar poetry came when the symptoms of the disintegration of this intensity began to appear. What the postwar poets began to suffer then was a lack of intense experience, an oppression of mass production, and the diffusion of poetic themes. Poets suddenly found themselves in the labyrinth of economic over-production and commercialism after violence, starvation, and suicidal devotion. This was a tremendously drastic change. People are becoming paralyzed and apathetic in the mass society, and although poets feel crazed with bitterness they cannot yet discern whether this change is structural or not, and rather feel completely dismayed in the new situation—a rare one in modern Japan. For in the process of Japanese modernization there has never been such a long peaceful term as the one since 1945. Always modern Japan was involved in wars, or rather I must say Japan kept on invading Asian countries, anachronistically imitating Western imperialism. Although modern Japanese intellectuals resisted this tendency, their proposals were all defeated. Not a few committed suicide. If not, they converted—converted not into another belief, but rather into aestheticism.

But if we look back to the premodern age, Japan had more than 250 years of peaceful isolation under the Tokugawa shogunate. And poets, like the anonymous Senryu poets, who belonged to the common people and contributed 17 syllabled satirical verses to the compiler Karai Senryu (1718–90), had to and could endure the staleness of society, yet produce a kind of creative writing. So if we see the Japanese cultural situation from afar, it is the history of long isolation and sudden interference, the sad repetition of the colonial mind and chauvinism, and the peculiarly imcomprehensible uniqueness. Can poetry be unrelated to this? I don't think it is possible.

Japanese language itself is considered to be very isolated, and yet inside the country it is an integral part of life and can be understood well anywhere, although there have been numerous dialects. As for the way of inscribing, it absorbed and digested foreign words through its peculiar way of adaptation, especially from the Chinese. For example, poems were written in Chinese from ancient times in Japan, but these poems in Chinese were recited completely differently from the way they were in China.

In the present Japanese language, Chinese characters are used together with two kinds of Japanese phonograms (Hiragana and Katakana) mixed, and Chinese characters (Kanji), which have more than one pronunciation usually but have not yet lost some essential charm to the poets as ideas or as things visualized. This mixed use of ideograms and phonograms at the same time is undoubtedly peculiar in itself. I think this may be very dogmatic, but I want to say from my poetic preoccupation that this mixed use through adaptation has some curious coincidence with religious syncretism in Japan, which appears unbelievable for Westerners, but very natural for Japanese. People believe at the same time in Shintoist Gods, Buddhism, and Confucianism. In everyday life these are combined and embodied in numerous rituals. From the Western theological point of view the Japanese attitude cannot be called religious, but rather too worldly. However, from the Japanese point of view, Western Monotheism is after all connected with that other world—the absolute one—which is a little bit too absurd for contemporary living. So in the contemporary age this syncretism can be the way to be worldly-wise about everything crucial, for good or for evil. And this mixed use, or peaceful coexistence of the various opposing elements, can be seen in every sphere of Japanese cultural life.

Mixture, but not thorough permeation. Transformation after transformation, and yet hard-core preservation. Noh, Kabuki, and the modern theatre. Japanese and Western paintings. Music of traditional, Western classical, and Jazz. They are existing altogether without mutual thorough inter-penetration. About poetry, traditional or modern *tanka* and *haiku* poets are seemingly very indifferent to contemporary free verse, and vice versa. These forms do not dominate each other, and one cannot extinguish the others. Of course, historically *tanka* originated first and was long preserved as a court poetry, and *haiku* came second and spread most widely. The fact that these three kinds of poetic forms can exist, and generally do not interfere with each other, also shows the symptoms of the Japanese cultural situation. I could not find an adequate word, so I am calling this a peaceful coexistence. It is well known that the two short traditional forms have definite regulating devices, but modern Japanese poetry does not have any such lasting regular form. It is free. In the prewar age at the time (1882) of the so-called Shin Tai Shi (the new-styled poetry) some forms of longer repetitive use of 5–7 or 7–5 syllables were about to become standard, but they could not because of their monotonousness. These two fundamental syllabic lines, which derived from classical *tanka* and *haiku*, can be seen now in popular lyrics—full of clichés. Modern poets, who want to put the importance upon the sounds and rhythms of their poetry, make use of some regular phonetic forms, and sometimes invent their own with much experimentation. But as a whole modern Japanese poetry has no regular forms at all—it is completely free— poets must find their own form each time they begin to write: "organic form."

Of postwar poetry, I mentioned only three groups, simply not to confuse readers, but actually there were innumerable groups, many of them publishing their own magazines. In one of the three monthly poetry magazines, "Gendaishi Techo" (Notebook of Contemporary Poetry), in its annual December issue a list of some 1,700 poets' addresses is made public. Among this number no *tanka* and *haiku* poets are included. But it should be noted here that on the other hand no major Japanese publisher takes the trouble to produce books of poems from among these numerous poets. The reading of modern poetry has not yet become popular, even though some trials or experimentations are occasionally made. (But annually in January in the emperor's court *tanka* recitation is held. Amateur *tanka* poets whose works have been accepted gather and hear their own *tankas* recited like an ancient ritual: an example of *hard-core preservation.*)

Two reasons, I think, may be mentioned why poetry reading cannot be popular in Japan. Modern poetry reading is actually surrounded not only by those who like *tanka* and *haiku*, but also by those who are pleased with Shigin (peculiar recitation of Chinese poems in Japanese), Rokyoku (sentimental epic recitation about gamblers and outlaws), and Kabuki declamations. Of course, these latter are not called poetry in the modern sense, but rather fall into the general category of entertainment: music with words. In any case, it should be noted that the way of recitation is well-preserved and does not show any signs of disappearing. Even though all these forms differ widely, in their concept of poetry, from the work of contemporary poets, they do have an impact on the auditory sense of the general public.

One more important thing is that contemporary poets use the ideogram Kanji (Chinese characters) very frequently to make their images precise and rich. And these ideograms are understood at once when seen like hieroglyphics, but sometimes misunderstood when pronounced. So it can be said that many contemporary poems are much more understandable when they are seen than when they are read aloud.

Consequently, modern Japanese poetry as a whole is cut off from vital colloquial expressions, but in exchange for this it can seek clear and subtle images full of sensitive feelings and the association of ideas—not with logic, but with seemingly arbitrary imagery. And this association of ideas and images, if it can have some consistency or enduring power, is the keynote of Japanese poetry. Recently some postwar poets have become keenly aware of the unrecitableness in the Japanese language of the above described poems, and are making many experiments to broaden the range of poetry and reach for a larger audience by breaking the barriers of conventional poetic idioms.

To prepare an anthology of living authors is always very difficult, especially so when the editor wants to make it representative and comprehensive. And it is much more difficult if the anthology is in translation. For example the poems with language experiments in sound are untranslatable. Although the remaking might be successful in the second language, whether the result would be equivalent with the original is quite doubtful. Therefore, the poems with language experiments in imagery—that is, those which acquired a new field or area for our inner imaginative living—and the poems which contained some substantial discovery about this hard life itself were my preference. But this is, I think, only the tip of an iceberg. Under the sea of untranslatability there are sparkling elements hidden almost forever. To see the light there, all you can do is to learn the original language—one of the most isolated modern languages in the world.

Iowa City and Tokyo, 1974

HADAKA NO GENGO: The Naked Language of Postwar Japanese Poetry

Roy Andrew Miller

The foreign reader of Japanese literature in translation necessarily approaches his subject under the limitations of a built-in disability; significant difficulties are interposed between him and his translated texts by the form and nature of the Japanese originals themselves. Usually he is unable to control those originals, and hence he is totally at the mercy of the translator. He cannot verify what may have been done to the originals to make them palatable—or at the very least understandable—to him; and this of course is hardly a very satisfactory situation for either the appreciation or the enjoyment of literature. It is necessary, but it is not satisfactory.

In the case of the modern, post-World War II poetry from Japan translated in this volume, the problem is a double one, almost as if two, rather than one, foreign language had interposed itself between the foreign reader and his translated texts. One of these languages is of course simply the Japanese in which these poems are written, but the other is something a little more involved than any "natural language," to borrow some of the jargon of the computer people. It is something difficult to illustrate, and at best may be rather lamely explained as being the complex set of relationships existing between the Japanese of these poems and the conventional language of traditional Japanese poetry.

The poets responsible for these poems write of course in the former; but both they and their readers, their Japanese readers in

Japan, read and interpret these poems against the common, given, and (in Japan at least) universally understood background of that other language—the involute and involved conventional diction and expression of the traditional Japanese poetic forms that the modern poets in this volume have turned their back on. Since, in this sense at least, not one but two foreign languages interpose themselves between the reader of these translations and the Japanese originals, the task of the translators whose work appears in this volume has been doubly difficult.

It is difficult to illustrate this situation with easily understandable examples from other fields, but perhaps some effort in that direction will be better than none. If one were to learn the German language initially and entirely from the libretti that Richard Wagner wrote for his music dramas, he would end up not only with a highly unusual vocabulary, syntax, and style (not to mention frightening the wits out of anyone he might meet on a visit to Germany!), but much more importantly, he would in the process have rendered himself virtually immune to just those special features of Wagner's poetic style and diction which are most important because of the very fact of their deviation from normal German. The English speaker who approaches the language of the *Ring* must penetrate the barriers of two foreign languages—normal German, and the language of Richard Wagner's libretti. This example will perhaps help to illustrate at least some of the problems that the language of these modern Japanese poems present for their translators, although the perceptive reader will by this time have noted that in the German example the terms of reference are almost completely reversed in terms of the Japanese materials that we are trying to elucidate. One is tempted to venture another example that is probably a little farfetched, but that also may make an important point. For some years now, the New York stage has at least been enlivened, if not particularly edified, by a series of reviews featuring frontal nudity and exhibitions of simulated sex acts; the genre of course began with *Oh! Calcutta!* and has continued through many imitative spin-offs of that pioneer piece (the most recent of which, at this writing, is engagingly entitled *Let My People Come*). Whatever dramatic statement these theatrical adventures may make surely is predicated upon the fact that most people do not walk around unclothed, or engage in sex acts, either simulated or for real, in public view; but there is still another level to all this, and one more significant for our present discussion. The more important point is not what people do in daily life, but what people generally do on the stage. The theatre-goer knows that people in plays and reviews do not generally carry on in that fashion; and it is in these terms of striking contrast with accepted theatrical convention that *Oh! Calcutta!* and its epigonic avatars make whatever statement they may indeed accomplish. The reader of the kind of contemporary Japanese poetry translated in this volume finds himself in much the same situation as the audiences in the expensive first four rows of these sex-and-nudity reviews: his attention is forcibly engaged less by the fact of what he is being made to watch than by his realization that what he is being made to watch is spectacularly different from the accepted conventions for theatrical performances. The language of these poems, in terms of accepted Japanese literary and poetic traditions, is totally nude, unadorned, without a stitch; and the Japanese reader knows this. To say that the language of these poems represents a departure from the traditions of Japanese poetic diction is simply to cloud the issue with indirection; better to think of it as a violent stripping away of all protective covering, a hurried, compulsive urge to display as prominently as possible everything that is normally kept hidden in layers of involute linguistic devices; in a word, it is *hadaka no gengo*, "naked language." Naturally, all this imposes severe burdens upon the translator, but not upon him alone. It also makes it imperative for the reader of these translations

Miller • xxix

at least to make the attempt to put these poems, as far as possible, into that perspective *vis-à-vis* traditional Japanese diction and style against which they make their most effective poetic statement. And that is no easy task.

This is of course no place in which to attempt an instant introduction to the poetics of traditional Japanese literature, even if one were possible. But the reader of these translations who is not able to consult the Japanese originals at first hand, and who does not have some familiarity with the styles and techniques of the traditional poetic forms in Japan, is strongly urged to complement his reading in the present volume with some supplementary reading in and about the involved, fully-clothed poems of traditional Japan. Otherwise he runs the risk of approaching these pages somewhat as if he were a man just arrived from Mars who finds himself in a frontrow seat at *Oh! Calcutta!*, and who might very well not be in the least surprised at the goings-on, for the simple reason that he would not know that people on this planet do not always disport in public in that fashion, or in that condition.

Fortunately, one is able to recommend a solid, reliable, and most surprisingly of all, an interesting source for such information: *Japanese Court Poetry*, by Robert H. Brower and Earl Miner (Stanford University Press, 1961). Here the reader will find a full-scale treatment of traditional Japanese poetry, with romanized original texts accompanying many translations, and a wealth of detailed analysis and technical treatments that will provide him with the background he will almost surely need for reading the translations in the present volume. After he has learned, from Brower and Miner's pages, something of the involved technical-language devices of the traditional Japanese poet—the set poetic epithet or cliché (*makura kotoba*), the "pivot word" (*kakekotoba*), the "associated term" (*engo*), and initially at least the most mysterious of all these technical devices of traditional poetic language, the "preface" (*jo*)—then and only then will he be able to turn to the poems translated in this book and appreciate the impact and force of the literary statement that they make.[1] Then for the first time will he be able to see them for what it is that their original language, in Japanese, makes them: a naked statement, stark and unclothed in a context and in a "country" (by which I mean the "country" of Japanese poetic tradition) where elaborate, involved, and incredibly multi-layered diction is the rule and not the exception. The language of these poems itself—and by and in itself—rips everything away, lays bare things not normally visible within the structure and diction of the Japanese literary tradition, and allows nothing to be hidden or reserved as private or secret. *Oh! Calcutta!*—Oh! Tokyo!

Of all the different special demands that these poems make upon their translators—and hence also, by implication, upon the readers of these translations—the most important (and the most difficult to overcome successfully) surely are those in the area of the special diction and the resulting unique texture of these lines. Professor Kijima Hajime in his own introduction to this volume, manages to sum up this problem quite neatly when he writes of the "history of long isolation and sudden interference" that characterizes Japanese literary and cultural history. Precisely the same combination of "long isolation and sudden interference" has characterized the history of the language, at least the history of the language viewed as a vehicle for aesthetic articulation. In these poems we find the end result (one wonders if it will, indeed, prove to be the "final result"?) of the most recent, and most powerful, upheaval and interference after the long placid years of reverie in isolation.

Miki Taku, in his poem *Adolescent Thought*, translated in full below, speaks in this connection for all the poets in this volume:

1 Some of these technical aspects of the 'decorative language' of traditional Japanese poetry are described and illustrated in my book *The Japanese Language* (Chicago: University of Chicago Press, 1967), p. 298 ff., which the reader who is not able to use Japanese-language sources may find useful.

hora goran yo boku no	hey! look here! my organism
oruganisumu wa	demands
kotoba wo yōkyū shite iru dare	words words that can be
ni demo	
tsutawaru kotoba . . .	communicated to everybody . . .[2]

Traditional Japanese poetry would not even admit long-since naturalized Chinese loanwords into its refined and precisely limited parameters of diction, consciously limiting itself to the lexical resources of the native Japanese vocabulary. With these modern poets, all this caution has been swept aside. Their need for expression demands words, words, words, and their demands can be met only by bringing into play not only the full totality of the modern Japanese lexical store, in which the native inheritance is already fleshed out by thousands and thousands of Chinese loanwords, but also by the lexical potential of other languages as well—particularly of English and of French. Miki, in the fragment cited above, uses a foreign term for "organism" not because he could not have said the same thing in Japanese, but in order to make a very special kind of statement and to express precisely what the portion or segment of his being it is that makes these extraordinary lexical demands: the words, words, words that his "organism" will be demanding, and that the "organisms" of the modern Japanese poets in general continue to demand in these pages, have been, like his "organism," boldly ripped away from the traditional sheath of Japanese culture and letters. They can no longer find adequate expression within the

2 The translations that I have included with the romanized text examples in this introduction are nothing more than literal English renderings presenting an idea of what the Japanese text says, on the simplest, most elementary level of meaning. The reader who knows Japanese will, and should, ignore them, since the romanized Japanese on the left-hand side of the page says the same thing. These English versions aim simply at helping the reader who does not know Japanese make something out of the examples cited; he may also find it profitable to compare these simple, literal versions with those of the poet-translators in the body of the volume. I have attempted to keep these literal English versions line-for-line parallel with the originals, but of course this has not always been possible, because of the great structural and syntactic differences between the two languages.

limits of the Japanese vocabulary, rich though it may be, anymore than one can fight one's way onto a crowded Tokyo bus or subway successfully if burdened with the long, confining skirt and trailing sleeves of a traditional Japanese *kimono*, no matter how rich and satisfying its fabric and lines may be. These poets cry for words, words, words that can be "communicated to everyone," and this in itself determines that a large, and important, layer of their diction necessarily involves foreign, non-Japanese expressions as well as coined native lexical items that often strike the reader of the originals as still only half-naturalized. With all this the best translator in the world can, of course, do very little. Miki's employment of *oruganisumu* (which incidentally shows by its form in Japanese that it is borrowed not from English "organism" but from French "organisme") sets a texture for the passage at which, no matter how skillful the translator, a reader unable to refer to the original will probably not even be able to guess.

Like everything else in life and letters, all this can be, and often indeed is, carried too far. The ultimate aesthetic goal of all this wholesale taking-over of non-Japanese words into the diction of poetry is, precisely as Miki puts it, to evolve a poetic language that "can be communicated to everybody." No one is more sensitive to his cultural and intellectual isolation within the larger world community than the modern Japanese man or woman of letters, scratching away with fountain pen on ruled manuscript paper in his cumbersome script, and hoping always to be able to write for, and to be read by, mankind, while realizing that he is fortunate indeed if even a literate Japanese is ever fully able to figure out what he means to say. What begins as an effort to facilitate communication, in the larger sense of that word, through lifting the sights of Japanese poetry up and above the limits of its inherited lexical materials, too often produces a texture of borrowings and half-naturalized terms so dense as to result at last in a thicket of virtual imcomprehensibility.

Miller • xxxiii

Here too, it is an unfortunate fact that the translator can generally do little or nothing to communicate this to the reader: to translate is by its nature to clarify, straighten out, and rationalize. Too often, in the translation of modern Japanese poetry, this must end up being done to lines that are, in the original, intentionally (or at least inevitably) unclear, misshaped, and anything but rational.

Examples of what is meant here could be drawn from almost any poem translated in this volume, but Shiraishi Kazuko's work provides particularly clear materials. Perhaps this is because, as a poet of the Japanese diaspora (she was born in Vancouver) she is clearly a poet who is particularly vulnerable to these demands for "words that communicate to everybody." At the same time, as a diaspora poet, her response to these demands is often particularly striking. Her poem here translated as *My Tokyo* itself provides an excellent example of what we are talking about: the title of the poem, in the original Japanese text, appears just that way, in English, printed in roman letters, standing straight up-and-down on the page (in order to fit in with the Japanese text which is of course printed that way), and providing at the outset of the poem a touch of texture that is the despair of the translator. What is he supposed to do, when he puts the rest of the poem into English—put the title back into Japanese? Perhaps that would indeed communicate to the reader of the translation something of the diction of the original, but at best it would be a measure of desperation, and at the very least simply puzzle the reader beyond all point. Better to leave it alone, which is what has been done here.

Ms. Shiraishi is one of the many poets represented in this volume who herself responds to this problem in a fashion that will seem, to many students of traditional Japanese life and literature, quite characteristic: she often provides running glosses and commentaries for her readers (her Japanese language readers, of course), explaining what she is doing while she is actually doing it. Here too we are faced with a phenomenon of poetic diction about which the translator can do little or nothing. In the case of the poem that is here translated under the title of *Phallus*, Ms. Shiraishi's original title is a Sino-Japanese loanword, *dankon*, itself a somewhat unusual lexical item that she then glosses, in roman letters and in English, in the original text, as "(penis)." After this introduction to the problem, it will perhaps come as somewhat less of a surprise to find that later, in the body of the poem itself, such exotica as "Amen hotep" have been glossed for the Japanese reader ("an ancient king of Egypt," Ms. Shiraishi explains). Perhaps more interest should be attached to those instances where internal glosses might have been useful, and none are provided. Twice in this poem, she uses the foreign term *kosumosu*:

dankon wa hibi ni gungun sodachi	the phallus growing larger day by day
ima wa kosumosu no manaka ni haete . . .	now has grown in the heart of the (or a?) cosmos . . .
dankon ga	the phallus
ugokidashi kosumosu no wakiatari ni aru to	begins to move and when it is alongside the (or a?) cosmos
nagame ga yoi no da . . .	the view is great . . .

Precisely what the Japanese reader is expected to make of all this is anything but clear, and of course the translator into English must make up his mind one way or another—not for him the luxury of lexical indecision. In these passages *kosumosu* might be either "cosmos," the universe conceived as an orderly or harmonious system, or "cosmos," the name of the common tall garden herb of the aster family (both words are attested in modern Japanese texts, as it turns out, as early as 1909).[3] Either "cosmos" might very well be expected to be one of the "words that can be communicated to every-

3 For the earliest attestations of "cosmos" in Japanese texts, see Arakawa Sōbee, *Gairaigo jiten* [A dictionary of loanwords in Japanese] (Tokyo: Kadokawa shoten, 1972; 33rd ed.), p. 424.

body," and yet here—probably, I suspect, with full intention to do so—Ms. Shiraishi ends instead by puzzling everybody, Japanese reader, translator, and English reader alike. Her two fragments above work equally well with either sense of "cosmos," and one could almost accuse her of having here reverted to the "pivot-word" techniques of the traditional poets.

In the case of the work of Ms. Shiraishi, it is clear that such calculated mingling of several lexical levels,[4] notably through the introduction of exotic lexical materials, is to be understood as an involved metaphor for the Japanese diaspora itself: lexical and semantic displacement and skewing correspond most effectively and elegantly to the emotional and psychological displacement and skewing that the Japanese-Americans and Japanese-Canadians have endured over the past decades. But the technique is by no means limited to the work of poets who are themselves actually representatives of the North American diaspora. Perhaps this is because in a larger sense, all modern Japanese poets belong to the diaspora, and the diction of their work shows it, even though any individual poet may never physically have left Japan.

But modern Japanese poetic diction need not be studded with foreign lexical borrowings to achieve a totally un-Japanese texture. One of the most striking ways in which the same effect is achieved restricts itself solely to native, inherited Japanese vocabulary items,[5] and yet results in a texture that is, if anything, even more striking than the result of the introduction of any number of foreign terms—more striking, because it is able to pervade long expanses of

4 The reader interested in this subject who cannot avail himself of the enormous Japanese-language literature may find at least an introduction to the system of "levels of speech" (*keigo*) and its problems in modern Japanese in *The Japanese Language*, p. 269 ff.

5 The treatment in Marleigh G. Ryan, *Japan's First Modern Novel* . . . (New York: Columbia University Press, 1967), especially p. 42 ff., of the language of modern Japanese fiction, and of its evolution at the hands of the literary pioneers of the Meiji period, particularly Futabatei Shimei (1864–1909), cannot fail to interest the student of the language of the poems translated in this volume.

syntax, and hence its effects are not dissipated on the level of the individual lexical item.

This technique, which again of course leaves the translator helpless, is particularly noticeable in the frequent introduction of pronouns and overt plural references into the diction of these poems.

In the case of pronouns, the poets are not only flying in the face of traditional Japanese style but are also violating that insistence upon non-personification that lies at the heart of so much Japanese writing and thought. The strident insistence of these poets on making clear to the reader that the speaker is "I," their constant hammering away at overt references to "you" and "he" and "she," is all, in the originals, so thoroughly un-Japanese as to leave with the Japanese reader the impression—which is quite correct, in this case—that he is being forced, once and for all, to make all the decisions of personification that in traditional Japanese writing, poetry and prose alike, need not be made; and indeed, are not supposed to be made.

Here the translator of these poems finds himself in very deep waters indeed: not only are the repeated insistences upon "I," "you," "he," "she" and "they," so forceful and attention-arresting in the original, inevitably going to slip unnoticed into their normal expected places in his English lines, but he also lacks any technique in English for coping with the lexical *embarras des richesses* strewn in his way with such a lavish hand by the Japanese pronoun with its profligate categories. How is the translator to distinguish between formal, male *watakushi* "I," friendly, peer-group male *boku* "I," rough, joking-relationship-oriented male *ore* "I," etc., etc.—not to mention all the female reflexes of this same elaborate system of personal-reference terms within the overall structuring of the "levels of speech" phenomenon of modern Japanese. Ms. Shiraishi begins her *My Tokyo* with the following:

Miller • xxxvii

watashi wa shakuson no yō	Like the Buddha himself I
ni	
hotondo kono toshi ni suwari	sit more or less in this city
ima 10-gatsu no buryō wo	and now have conceived a ten-
kainin shite iru . . .	month ennui . . .

Her initial statement in this highly personal poem is, quite fittingly, in the form of the female first-person pronoun *watashi*, a word that is not only overtly marked with respect to the sex of the speaker, but one that also has definite if difficult-to-describe adumbrations on the "levels-of-speech" scale. For this pronoun to appear in poetic diction at all is a striking, and significant, feature of the poem; and that the poet has chosen this particular form of the pronoun represents another and higher level of significant aesthetic decision. The translator can, in his despair, only write "I." The strident lesbian tone of Tomioka Taeko's *The Girlfriend* may even be overlooked by the reader of the translation, but to the Japanese reader of the original it is blatantly expressed by means of the introduction of the extremely intimate female first-person pronoun *atashi*, a form that brings to its simple lexical-level significance of "I" added intimations of carressing intimacy at which the translator can only hope to hint:

inaka no yado de	In a country inn
atashi wa kanojo no	I first managed to muss up
burijitto barudō no yō na	her neatly arranged hair-do
moridakusan no kami-no-ke	just like
wo	
hajimite kakimushiru koto	Brigitte Bardot's . . .
ga dekite . . .	

The second line of the fragment quoted is the heart of the matter here: *atashi wa kanojo no*, literally, "I," followed by the topic-subject marker, then *kanojo* "she," followed by the possessive-referent particle. It is no accident that here this entire line is devoted to the manipulation of these overt pronominal references. In traditional Japanese literary expression, neither pronoun would be either necessary nor desirable. By using them here, the poet forces us into accepting her own personification, and (particularly with the use of the intimately female form *atashi*) forces us, whether we wish it or not, into intimate recognition of the fact of her lesbianism. At the same time, the stridently personal identity of her homosexual partner is also impressed upon us with equal force by the (in Japanese linguistic terms) totally unnecessary reference to *kanojo* "she." This passage would be perfectly clear in Japanese without either of these overt pronominal references, and in almost any other variety of written Japanese, it would have neither. When these pronouns appear, as they do here, they mean something particular and special, as they clearly do in this particular fragment.

Equally beyond the grasp of the translator is the frequent employment of overt grammatical plurals in these poems, often in conjunction with the pronouns. Though traditional Japanese is by no means lacking in linguistic devices by means of which it is able to specify plural number when it wishes or needs to, the singular-plural grammatical category is not an obligatory one, and hence overt number-reference is never an automatic feature. It is used if and when it appears at all as a conscious, overt device. This is true in general terms of the language in all periods and in all its literary manifestations; and it is particularly true of the poems translated in this volume. When we find, for example, *kimitachi*, "you" (pl.), we may be sure that the poet has used this collocation for a specific reason; and the same is true of such very un-Japanese looking expressions as *kamitachi*, "the gods," where we can almost see the poet grappling with the highly undifferentiated, amorphous, and thoroughly non-anthropomorphic conceptualization of deity and divine personages in traditional Japanese thought. He is anxious lest what he writes be taken in the old Japanese fashion, as *kami*, "god" or "gods" or "godhead" or "divinity" or just about anything nonhuman, and so he writes instead *kamitachi*, an overtly marked plural that is almost precisely English "gods." But there is an important difference between *kami* and *kamitachi* that no translation can ever approximate: the translation of *kamitachi* is a perfectly ordinary English collocation, while its Japanese original is strikingly exotic, and specifically designed to sound, and to be, un-Japanese.

The manipulation of pronouns represents the conscious employment of inherited Japanese lexical distinctions for the poets' ends; the overt employment of plurals is something a little different, since it so obviously looks in the direction of English and other modern European languages where (totally unlike Japanese) the singular-plural category is an obligatory distinction. From the combination of these two devices, it is only a short step until we have reached the very foreign-looking, and at times almost totally asyntactic Japanese, that distinguishes a significant number of the poems translated in this volume. Several of the translators have displayed remarkable resourcefulness in devising unusual English in order to reproduce unusual Japanese; but the fact of the matter is that English is, in this respect, a language that is simply less willing to be pulled and prodded out of shape than is Japanese. Any line of English poetry that had undergone the grammatical and syntactic displacements that distinguish much of the poetry in this volume would not only no longer be poetry: it would long ago in the process have ceased to exist even on the level of intelligible language.

Japanese, perhaps because of the inherent richness of its grammatical apparatus, can suffer a surprising total of amputations and unnatural regraftings within its structure without totally expiring as a viable organism. Grammatical particles and markers can be omitted; normal syntactic patterns rearranged into novel and striking orders that never occur naturally in the language; whole sequences of grammatical government can be turned inside-out, without interfering seriously with the understanding of the Japanese reader—upon whom, at the same time of course, the cumulative aesthetic effect of these major displacements and violations of expected order is tremendous. To attempt anything even close to this either with original English materials or with an English translation of one of these Japanese originals is to risk total unintelligibility.

As with so much else in Japanese culture, these syntactic and grammatical displacements are often carried out within the physical constraints of what must be called, even by the most generous estimate, an extremely limited universe. Kora Rumiko's *She* provides a striking example within only five very short lines:

sukoshizutsu kanojo wa wasureru	Little by little she forgets:
kokyō wo	home-town
hanakotoba wo	the language of flowers
umi wo	the sea
hōkō wo . . .	roaming . . .

The reader will by this time himself be familiar enough with the problems presented by the special language of modern Japanese poetry to realize that the *kanojo* "she" in the opening line of this fragment is no ordinary lexical item, but rather one that involves specifically overt personification. But over and above that feature, everything else about this fragment is also totally un-Japanese, in terms of conformity to normal grammatical and syntactic norms. Each of the last four lines cited, ending with the direct-object particle *wo,* should precede, not follow, the verb *wasureru* "forgets"; Japanese objects precede the verbs that govern them. The word-order here is totally foreign, and totally English. The translation can be accurate, and pleasing, and read well, and still convey no sense at all of the tension and sense of interrupted rhythm that permeate the original lines. The closer the original flow and ordering of the Japanese original has been displaced by the poet in the direction of English, the closer to normal, natural, even to poetic, English will be an accurate, literal translation. But by precisely the same token, the resulting English, pleasing, accurate, and literal though it may be, will necessarily give little if any hint of the stylistic texturing of the original out of which it grew. It is all so difficult, it hardly seems fair.

Displaced, disarranged Japanese syntax, and violation of grammatical norms carried to the point of linguistic rapine, are all beautifully illustrated by one of the poems in this volume that I personally happen to consider to be one of the most effective single poems included in this collection, Hasegawa Shiro's hauntingly evocative *The Cat*. Whether I feel this way about this particular poem because of its style and expression, both of which are striking, or simply because in my time in Japan I have found myself foster-parent to so many wandering cats, is anything but clear; at any rate, the poem is remarkable enough on any one of several levels—including the way in which it illustrates the linguistic point last made above—to allow the luxury of citation in full:

1 *nossori kita neko ga shōnen no*	The big, fat cat showed up in the young man's
iru kashiya ni, nureen to chiisana niwa	rented house, tiny porch and cramped garden
miruku wakete shōnen yatta	the young man shared his milk with the cat
burun burun burun burun	'purr, purr, purr, purr'
5 *choku choku sore kara neko kita*	after that the cat often showed up
nureen de hinatabokko	to snooze in the sun on the tiny porch
miruku wakete shōnen yatta	the young man shared his milk with him
yonaka ni amado no, mukō	in the middle of the night beyond the shutters
sunoa sunoa sunoa sunoa	'snore, snore, snore, snore'
10 *ibiki tatete neko neteta*	the cat snored as it slept on

asa ni miruku, shōnen yatta	mornings, the young man shared his milk with him
aru hi, neko konakatta	one day the cat did not show up
dō shita no kana,	I wonder what happened to him, the
shōnen itta	young man said
mo sore'kkiri	and from then on
15 *nossori neko, konakatta*	the big, fat cat never showed up again
nanajūnen keika	A Lapse of Seventy Years—
shōnen hachijissai	the young man is 80 years old
betsu no machi, betsu no kashiya	in another town, another rented house
morutaru apāto	a concrete apartment building
20 *shōnen shinda shinu toki itta*	the young man died: when he died he said
ano neko, dō shita no kana	I wonder what ever happened to that cat

One hardly knows where to begin in pointing out all the displacements from usual, ordinary Japanese that distinguish the language of this poem. To begin with, the Japanese reader is first of all struck by the fact that almost none of the grammatical particles, the syntactic life-blood of the language, have survived intact, except for the subject-marker *ga* in line 1, which as a result stands out all the more strikingly because of the absence of so much else of the expected grammatical equipment in the following twenty lines. In line 1 also, *nossori* "big, fat, substantial (of animals)" goes directly with *neko* "cat" in sense, and should also go with it syntactically more directly than it does here; by moving the verb *kita* "came, showed up" into the place it here occupies, separating the other two, the poet immediately gives notice of his intention to communicate with us in asyntactic, stripped-down Japanese of the most unusual sort; and he is fully as good as his word. What would be the usual syntactic order for line 2 is here totally reversed. In line 3 we find that only the nouns and verbs have survived, and in a strikingly unorthodox order at that, with all the grammatical particles stripped away in the process: for the poet's *miruku wakete shōnen yatta* ordinary Japanese would have *shōnen ga miruku wo wakete yatta*. Gone are the *ga* marking the subject (which ends up at the end, instead of the beginning), and the *wo* marking the direct object (which is similarly displaced). Lines 4 and 9 (and to some extent also the first two words of line 5) employ a Japanese literary device of hoary antiquity, *ad hoc* coinages of sound-imitative words, but this time with a difference, for this cat, as we could have guessed, is none of your ordinary Japanese felines. It not only snores in English (the repeated *sunoa* of line 9 is simply the English word "snore"), but it also purrs in the same foreign language (*burun*, line 4), since an ordinary, prosaic, and thoroughly Japanese cat says *gorogoro* when it purrs. (Japanese cats, I have been told more than once *in situ*, envy in phonetic helplessness the ability of their foreign cousins to get the flesh of their lips down over those difficult teeth and pronounce the initial labials of *miaow* and *purr*; Japanese cats must generally content themselves with the far less demanding *niau* and *gorogoro*. Wherever this cat in Hasegawa's poem comes from, he clearly has been around.) Every line in this poem is full of equally striking employment of conscious deflection, on the part of the poet, of normal Japanese syntactic and grammatical devices, but perhaps enough has already been said to make the point. By line 15, Hasegawa is content to allow the expected alliteration of the *n*'s in *nossori neko* to come together at last, having riveted at least a portion of our attention on this very point ever since the start of the poem by the asyntactic interpolation of the verb *kita* into this collocation in line 1. The consequent relaxation of tension involved in this long awaited resolution of anticipated alliteration is a signal that the poem is almost complete. Lines 16 and 19 rivet the attention by the introduction, without a word of warning, of lexical materials totally foreign to the otherwise thoroughly Japanese lexical stock of the

xliv •

poem (an apparent exception, but actually one that only goes to prove the rule, is provided by the *miruku* "milk" of lines 3, 7, and 11—nor is the neatly balanced separation of its appearances here in progressively farther and farther distant odd-numbered lines the result of sheer chance!). Line 16 is entirely in Sino-Japanese, as if it were the heading of a chapter in a book or a title in block letters spliced into a silent movie; and line 19 is, the observant reader of the romanized text above will (perhaps) have noticed already, in English in the original (literally, "mortar apart [ment]," meaning a building not made of traditional Japanese materials but rather of Western-style construction). The final *itta* "he said" of line 20 is sprung completely out of its normal syntactic position; and the final *kana* of the last line (which earlier appears in the same sense in the middle of line 13) is of considerable interest also. On a superficial level this word is simply a compound of the interrogative particle *ka* with the sentence-final dubitive particle *na*, the two together meaning something like "I wonder . . . ," but at the same time, the coincidence in form (if not in sense) of this compound with the canonical *kana* "Ah! . . ." of traditional Japanese poetry is, once more, hardly sheer chance. Imitating as he does here the forms and even the structure of traditional poetry with these completely colloquial, and completely asyntactic, materials, Hasegawa manages to erect something totally new upon the ruins of his knowledge of the older tradition, at the same time that he holds that tradition up to the glare of a contrast so merciless as to approach internal, if not self-parody.

We began above by presenting the language of these poems as stripping-away of all the customary decorations and embellishments of traditional Japanese poetics; a brief consideration, in conclusion, of what may very well be their single most salient structural feature—the great freedom and variety displayed by the poetic line that they employ—will, in a sense, bring us full circle. In one respect these poems contrast with the "received" poetic canons of Japanese taste more in this respect than in any other, for nothing is as rigorously integral to the traditional poetry than the rigidly determined number of feet in each line, five's and seven's alternating with each other according to a small number of well-known, and extremely rigid, patterns.

Here, of course, all that has been swept away with a vengeance. Sometimes, as in Tomioka Taeko's *Chairs*, the poetic line shrinks until it is, for all practical considerations, no more than the necessary syntactic minimum of noun plus accompanying grammatical particle:

takusan no	A beach where
marui tōisu no okareta	many
umibe wo	round rattan chairs had been placed
shashin de mita koto ga aru	I once saw in a photograph

At other times, as in Iwata Hiroshi's *Tyranny*, the line grows longer and longer, until it is finally itself totally abandoned as form, and as such, merges imperceptibly into long prose interludes. These prose interludes make their statement concerning the turning upside down of traditional Japanese poetry, and denuding it, the better to expose its workings to the gaze of all, in the most effective single way possible—by not even bothering to pay lip service to what have by this time become little more than typographical conventions of poetic forms.

These prose interludes are, of course, intimately connected with the prose lists of the "Neo-Perceptionists" (Shin kankaku-ha), and they point in two different directions—the almost stream-of-consciousness prose of much of the modern Japanese novel on the one hand, and the prose-poetry of the rhythmic exhaustive lists (*tsukushi*) of traditional Japanese literature on the other. To follow up either of these hints in any significant way would at once take us beyond the limits of these pages, but both must be laid under contribution if we are to understand fully the significance, within the world of Japanese language and letters, of those passages in these modern poems that appear in the originals—and are here translated—simply as prose. In some ways, perhaps, those passages present the greatest single challenge to the translator of anything in the present volume. In most of the other passsages, the translator at least has had the consolation of knowing that if nothing else typographical convention is on his side, but here even that solace abandons him. The Japanese are old hands at writing poetry as if it were prose; the English-language translator comes to it too late in his culture, if not too late in his life.

Difficult as they are both to translate and to read, these prose-appearing passages may very well be one of the most important aspects of all modern Japanese poetry, including the examples here presented to the English reader. This is because they provide us with clues of extraordinary value toward the solution of one of the great continuing mysteries in Japanese literary culture: the question that has been expressed neatly, if a little bluntly, along the following lines—"why did the Japanese until recently at least always write such short poems?" One very simple, and accurate answer, of course, is that they did not. The short poetic forms that we too often think of as characteristic of the Japanese poetic genius are short only when viewed entirely out of context, their natural and normal context being that of the sequence or anthology, where we now realize that they were arranged into systems of interrelated reference and fitted into patterns of integration and association that constituted another—and a vast—poetic structure in and of themselves. There really were no short poems in the history of Japanese literature, there were only short pieces of enormously larger wholes, whether those larger entities were anthologies and sequences, or the still larger contexts of prose works (with an enormous range here too, all the way from the *Tale of Genji* to Basho's *Narrow Road to the North*), or even larger—the immensely larger—contexts of entire poetic lives.

The other answer is somewhat less of a reply to the charge of triviality inherent in the traditional claim that the Japanese poetic genius found its typical, and most effective, expression, in tiny, short set pieces. It did not; and in evidence for this claim, and on this second level of disputation, we have the enormously long passages in rhythmic "prose" that distinguish an entire literature of historical romances and later stage works, ranging all the way from the aristocratic, elegant *Nō* texts to the blood, guts, and sex scenarios of the neo-Kabuki. Long after even the very structural principles of the integrated anthologies had been forgotten, and long after everyone had become bored and sick-to-death with playing at linked-verse chains, the theatre poets continued to go their own way, hand-in-hand with the story-tellers and other predecessors of the modern Japanese novel. If we were to ask where did traditional Japanese poetry go when it died, the answer is clear: it went back into prose, where in a sense it had often been; but the truth of the matter is that it never really died. And if the poems translated in this volume show nothing else, they certainly demonstrate the last statement with resounding conviction.

This may appear, at first glance, to have simplified the work of the translators of the poems in this volume, but actually it is the contrary that is true; for the logical consequence of all this is that to the well understood problems of translating Japanese poetry in the usual, traditional sense of that term, the translators of this book have also had to add much less well-understood problems of translating a kind of "poetic prose" very much akin to the language of much modern Japanese fiction. It is unfortunately impossible here to go into the details of the many ways in which the work of these poets—and the problems of their translators—run parallel to the work—and the translation problems—of modern Japan's novelists. In both instances, we find that the inherent possibilities of the original language have been enlarged, often to the breaking point. We find deformation of natural idiom. Some of this deformation is along the narrower lines illustrated above, but most of it takes place in wider, more comprehensive contours. We find an overpowering urge to work in terms of unintegrated, unorganized nominal collocations. These deformed expresssions are totally foreign to the normal syntactic flow of the language; moreover, they proudly eschew even the hesitant attempts that these poems occasionally make in order to bring them into the ordinary relationships of proposition and subordination.[6] Another related problem that must also await treatment elsewhere has to do with the fact that a significant number of the poets represented in this volume are themselves translators of modern European literature. Can anyone—and particularly any poet—ever be the same after having read French, German, and Russian and particularly after having translated them into a language as critically different in structure as Japanese is? I do not think so; and the problem is not only a problem for these poets, it is also a problem for their translators.[7] To cope with all these anomalies of language, and of linguistic structuring, and of syntactic ordering, and still produce an intelligible result that is at the same time a poem, is no mean feat. The extent to which the translators in this volume have succeeded can only be explained by the enormous *élan* of the originals. That this force proved sufficient to fuel them on their trajectory out of one culture and language into another is the best possible measure of the power of these poets, and of their work.

University of Washington, 1974

6 My debt here to Masao Miyoshi, *Accomplices of Silence, The Modern Japanese Novel* (Berkeley: University of California Press, 1974), particularly to his treatment of Kawabata Yasunari, p. 95 ff., will be obvious to any reader of his recent study of Japanese fiction.

7 The reader may also find relevant to this discussion my attempt at a theoretical treatment of the over-all problem of translation from Japanese, "On the difficulty of Japanese translation," pp. 469–478 in *Nihon bunka kenkyū ronshū* [Studies in Japanese Culture] (Tokyo: Japan P.E.N. Club, 1973), which also appears in Japanese translation as "Nihongo no hon'yaku no muzukashisa ni tsuite," pp. 324–331 in *Nihon bunka kenkyū kokusai kaigi gijiroku* [International Conference on Japanese Studies, Report] (Tokyo: Japan P.E.N. Club, 1973), vol. 2.

CONTENTS

THE POETRY OF POSTWAR JAPAN

Japanese names are given with family name first. Translators' names are in italics at the end of each poem.

SAGA NOBUYUKI 1902–

Born in Miyazaki Prefecture, Southern Japan. He was expelled twice from junior high school. Later, he was editor of the publishing house Bungeishunjusha. After World War II, he began to write poems, and has been editing the monthly poetry magazine *Shigaku* (Ars Poetica). *Counting Songs of Love and Death* was published in 1957.

FIRE

Never put out that fire again!
The tiny one from inside me I placed inside you.
It is the only one in the world;
the one picked up by a large bird
that flutters down the deep ravine
between death and me.
This tiny fire asks nothing of you.
It will protect you with the emptiness of zero.
It will not let anything injure you.
And now you stand naked, holding fire
on stairs going up endlessly.

Kijima

ON LOVING WOMEN

To love women
is to remake one woman's figure;
to confine her to a bunch of grapes;
to free her from death and crystal.

Give a quiet, marble pedestal
to the woman who can no longer stand straight,
her days exhausted with useless worry; suddenly,
on the stairs she thinks of something incredibly distant.

This evening, I am a tree in the garden, offering green to her.
Holding abundant time above me,
I stand with direct roots into life, a tree of love.

To love women
is to let one woman approach her true form,
constantly remaking her in the image of God.

Bean

THE MYTH OF HIROSHIMA

What are they looking for,
running to the summit of lost time?
Hundreds of people vaporized instantly
are walking in mid-air.

> "We didn't die."
> "We skipped over death in a flash and became spirits."
> "Give us a real, human death."

One man's shadow among hundreds is branded on stone steps.

"Why am I imprisoned in stone?"
"Where did my flesh go, separated from its shadow?"
"What must I wait for?"

The 20th century myth is stamped with fire.
Who will free this shadow from the stone?

Kijima

BONE

Since I had nothing to do,
I took off my skull.
Then I became incredibly sad.
Only two inches of white bone protruded from between my
   shoulders,
and occasionally it twitched.
There was no trace of my crazy love for women.
Birds no longer flew down to perch on it.
No one could hitch a tired horse from a far village to it.
Hurriedly, I put back my skull.
It landed with a dull rattle,
and settled back into its former position;
but since then, I can't forget that strange sound.

Kijima

ONO TOSABURO 1903–

Born in Osaka. He participated in the prewar avant-garde poetry movement and was once imprisoned. His book of criticism, *Shiron* (On Poetry), most of which was written during World War II, influenced the postwar generation. He brought many poets from Osaka, and has published twelve volumes of his own poems. *Fantastic Wish* was published in 1962.

NATIVE'S HANDS

In the Algerian desert
a guerrilla takes apart
his heavy machine gun.
My fingers have never loved one thing
so intelligently as his.
Close by him, an antelope, bearded like a saint,
stares at his hands' movement
with soft eyes.
Such a wise animal
has never wondered at my fingers.
At midnight, when I spread them
against the fluorescent light on my desk,
I see the veins translucence.
These are my hands.

Kijima

THE BURNING COOP

A small boat burns
in the middle of a river.
Actually, it is a coop burning on the boat.
No one is there.
Did they abandon the boat and swim ashore?
Did they die?
The burning coop spews out tongues of flame,
and smoke reaches high into the dusk.
Leaves flutter down, one after another,
from the tips of branches.

With the blast, an enormous object
passed overhead.
If there is a tree whose leaves have turned the color of a hearth,
what is their name for it?
Leaves float down
glittering with gold.

The heads of grass on the thatched roof
suddenly peel off,
and for a moment, they're blown one way.

The eves fall,
and a bit later
I see mud from the earthen walls quietly crumble.

The burning coop
still burns.

Kobayashi

AT THE FOOT OF TURQUINO

Placing the extracted,
blood-stained bullet
in his palm,
Guevara said, "It's out."
The peasant soldier nicknamed "Little Cowboy"
nodded slightly.
Teeth clenched,
he lay in a clump of grass
enduring the wound's pain.
The odor of blood and the odor of antiseptic
hung in the air.
In the distance
a sandstone cliff was lit with the setting sun
as if the world could take no other shape.
Guevara and Fidel and "Little Cowboy"
didn't think it strange
to find themselves in this kind of place.
Even when someone is wounded
or someone dies,
they look up at clouds
or turn their eyes toward trees.
They make friends with nature
differently than we do,
and nature befriends them.
Turquino is 1965 meters above sea level.
This mountain in the Sierra Maestra
is the tallest in Cuba.
Perhaps it's the same
as our country's Mt. Fuji.

Kobayashi

8 •

THE ENORMOUS FISH

A fish-monster
resembling a huge marlin
was pulled from the sea
and left on a vacant beach.
The monster vomitted out a bellyful of small fish,
and his own entrails, and died.
How horrifying!
How surprising
that the small fish had swallowed smaller ones.
The leaden sea glimmers,
appearing primeval.
What strange beasts the calm sea holds!
Although landed,
this one was unmanageable.
Half dried,
many years in desolation,
and still
it stinks of death.

Kijima

FROM THE WINTER OCEAN

Already
the turret,
and chimney, and mast,
are hacked off.
And the battleship's thirty-nine thousand ton hull
is still submerged,
red with rust, covered with oysters and barnacles.
No leaks in the deck.
The flooded sides and bottom
are tightly sealed.
All that's left
is to move in the pump
and connect the salvage tank.
Everything's ready!
Out of the winter sea white with waves
once again the huge form emerges.

Kobayashi

OGRE THISTLE

These fringes
and sharp thorns, the heavy corolla.
What a gigantic purple ogre thistle!
Did you really pick it?
The surrounding air is attacked by absolute dryness.
Where? Where was it blooming?
"Over there," is not enough.
Tell me where!
Can you see
the volcano?

Kijima

A FLOCK OF SPARROWS

a flock of sparrows
in the distance
in their flight
something constantly crackling
something constantly exploding
a harvest day's blood-like afterglow:
the earth reflected upside-down
in heaven

Kijima

HASEGAWA SHIRO 1909–

Born in Hokkaido. He was graduated from Hosei University. Later, he was captured in Siberia. A very prolific writer, he has novels, short stories, plays, and translations from Kafka to Brecht and Lorca to his credit. His collected works received the Mainichi Publication Prize. *Songs of Natives* was published in 1972.

BALLAD OF SOLDIERS

Take up your guitar and put it into tune.
Sing a song of soldiers all together now.
Hayohoi-hayohoi-hayohoi-hoi

Herded on a barnacled, bilge-water brig;
shipped out, waved goodbye, the soldier went to war.
Hayohoi-hayohoi-hayohoi-hoi

Oil-slicked ocean waves were his Waterloo.
His sea-sick carcass lay rolling in the brine.
Hayohoi-hayohoi-hayohoi-hoi

What's that shining there, in jungles deep and dark?
Wind worn skull and bones basking in the light.
Hayohoi-hayohoi-hayohoi-hoi

Still alive and breathing, the soldier disappeared—
Bricks on bricks had buried him, we heard from him no more.
Hayohoi-hayohoi-hayohoi-hoi

Liver, heart, kidneys, lungs, stomach, intestines,
blown to smithereens, he froze and decomposed.
Hayohoi-hayohoi-hayohoi-hoi

Spring came to the steppe and warm breezes, too.
Maggot maggot infested, the soldier slowly thawed.
Hayohoi-hayohoi-hayohoi-hoi

The days and nights of seven years came and went at last
And some of the soldiers made it home again.
Hayohoi-hayohoi-hayohoi-hoi

Some came home in packages bowed and neatly wrapped.
Boxed bones, rattle-rattle, tell-tale shake.
Hayohoi-hayohoi-hayohoi-hoi

Soap, socks, toilet paper's all we have to give,
In appreciation for the life you've had to live.
Hayohoi-hayohoi-hayohoi-hoi

Half his body left behind and half brought home again;
There he is, the human wreck, can't imagine where he's been!
Hayohoi-hayohoi-hayohoi-hoi

His repatriated half plays harmonica,
Sings ballads of the war and begs for its bread.
Hayohoi-hayohoi-hayohoi-hoi

A commuting businessman found him lying there—
It just so happens that the rush hour had begun.
Hayohoi-hayohoi-hayohoi-hoi

Laid out on a bench in front of the station,
The dead soldier
The dead soldier
The dead soldier . . .

Dead fingers welded to his harmonica,
Dead lips welded to his harmonica.
Hayohoi-hayohoi-hayohoi-hoi

Goodman

TRAVELLER'S SONG

What was it
half sunk half seen
bobbing in the sea
ahead of Columbus?
A leaf.
And what
did Noah's dove
sent a second time
bring back?
One soft olive leaf.
Before me on this sea:
a window
ink bottle old desk
newspapers.
Dove. Dove.
How many flights you've
flown for me. Again
now. Up. But
you'll come back
as usual
bringing nothing.

Fitzsimmons

WATCHMAN'S SONG

       High pressure low pressure
                   I
always wear
a raincoat   and wander
with a lantern   I
          am a watchman
   Faint trace of young animals
on the pavement   look
out virgins   I
know where these animals go
               I
         am the watchman
Lighting a lamp in the basement
of an empty building   every
one's gone home   I'm proud of
my lineage, watchmen all as
               I
         am a watchman
Negro soldier darker than night
walking by   I
can see   as you walk by
the white
bones inside you   I
         am the watchman
Sleeping   master
sleeping   everyone is
sleeping   and all is well
all's well for now   signed
              I
       the watchman

Fitzsimmons

SONG OF A CAT

A cat came slowly
To the boy's rented house
A tiny veranda and a tiny garden
He shared milk with the cat
tremble   tremble   tremble
The cat came again
Sat in the sun on the tiny veranda
The boy shared milk with it
At night beyond the shutters
Snore   snore   snore   snore
The cat snored in its sleep
Mornings the boy offered milk
But one day the cat didn't come
What happened   the boy said
Since then
The lazy cat hasn't come
70 years passed
The boy is 80 years old
In another town   in another rented house
Some stucco apartment building
The boy said as he died
How is that cat doing?

Kijima

SONG OF A RIBBON

A detailed statement
Of borrowing and lending
That's what I don't like
Much
Then what do you like
Well
Yes
Girls' laughter
Morning
A ribbon's brightness
A boat at sea
Still more
Yes
The fountain's whistle
You make
You
Whoever you are
And then
I like
The only summer
Which cannot be repeated

Kijima

SONG OF A PATIENT

Someone said
Your temperature's 170
Your eyes are green
Your tongue is all checkered
Yellow and black
You're sick
You're going to
Fade out
NO
I am my storm
I am my wreck
I am my deadlock
I am my drifting
I am the log to which I cling
And I am
My morning calm

Kijima

SUGAWARA KATSUMI 1911–

Born in Miyagi Prefecture, Northern Japan. He attended the Japan Art School. For activities in the anti-war movement during World War II, he was imprisoned. Presently, he makes his living as a designer. He edited *The Dictionary of Poetry*, and has published four volumes of poems. *Hands* was published in 1951.

OUR RESIDENCE

Believe what I believe.
This place we live.
A little fish you rip open.
Light inlaid upon scales.
Blue parsley on
an empty dish.
This is a day.
This is us.
Believe what I believe.
We cannot look ahead
unless we open a door.
I always feel that
morning came,
a day moved on,
night sank
as this weight on our hands.
Believe what I believe.
This residence is ours.
There is fire,

and sky,
and time also.
Darling,
at the bottom of things
incomparable and daily
we apprehend the width
of the Universe.

Kijima

"I AM ALONE, BUT WE ARE ALL"

I meet him
In the morning.
Then I become "we"
And two.
We meet them
On the tram-car,
And become a group.
The wind lifts up our songs,
Our flags and placards.
One group unites with another,
And again I
Change into a numberless "we."
I become a drop of a stream,
My thoughts, like sperm,
flicker around in the crowd.
Why am I so
Open-hearted today?
I think:
This air cleanses at its touch

My singularity.
I am one.
We are all.
The herald of time
Pursuing time changes
Runs around the earth.
Our voices echo even in Rio—
I think it's lovely;
It is autumn there,
While it is spring here.
The mane of a sandstorm in Kharakhorum desert,
White mountains sinking into Fjords.
It is summer here,
And winter over there.
I know: All the seasons
Of the world meet
On this day.
The varied races
All over the world
Make up a pattern of peoples.
I am one,
We are all.
I am jostled by people.
In a pocket surrounded
By the crowd
I cannot see anything
But the wide sky.
The sky lit by the sun
Now seems a sea,
Innumerable yachts waiting,
All their sails swelling.
Mosses stirring on the earth

Seem to stand still.
Single voices no longer
Reach us
Except with the louder tone.
And I feel
Myself expand and fuse into
The harmonious voices
Of our class.
I am one,
We are all.
When the enormous bellows
With tens of thousands
Of open valves
Resound high
Blowing
Blowing up through
Light-blue space,
We all now step
Freshly into
The first day of May.

Kijima

MITSUKO

That young girl who sang well
twenty years ago
became my bride twelve years ago.
A cheerful girl in a pink woolen dress.
You're still plump and cheerful
as if fate passes you by.

However we fail
your good intentions cancel all debts.
No matter what troubles we have
you believe they will be solved.
Affirming the future of cheerfulness
is your foremost virtue.
That has been a light in our long poor life.

Why are you so cheerful?
Do you believe in me
or in our life?
At times I look at you curiously,
but your plump body slowly walks the streets
and your laughter is like
that girl in the pink woolen dress.

Ayusawa

POET'S MOURNING

Someday I'll die.
(I hope it falls
on my favorite summer evening.)
Then all the poems I've written
would become suddenly alive.
The ancient organ my mother left,
the girl who brought in workday clothes
in a drizzle,
the chair which fell down with me
in the interrogation room of the police station,
and dead Dali who had a narcissus
planted over his skull,
they will all come
alive.
My wife will be there as well.
And Dali will run around
in the wheat field where the wind shines
and will be scolded
by our neighbor, Uncle Heihachi.

Someday, when I die
come out little poems
and dance joyously hand in hand
with pink lotus flowers,
the way your master wished
who in life loved
only gaiety.

Ayusawa

HANDS

These hands protected me from the police.
In winter, on the cold concrete floor
of the jail,
these hands brushed my falling hair.
These hands had been waiting many years
for me to come back;
they made solemn notes with a pipe
I used to hear.

My mother
the aged hands

One day when the double cherry blossoms
were falling, and the swallows sang
unsettling late spring's heavy air,
I went back home to hold those hands.
I was crying and I held in my own hands
thin wrinkled hands
which transferred their last shivering to me.
The hands of my mother
who is dying of sickness,
of weakness,
was never rewarded for anything.
I was warming her hands with mine
as if this would be my mother's
only reward.

Ayusawa

ISHIHARA YOSHIRO 1915–

Born in Shizuoka Prefecture, Middle Japan. He graduated from the Tokyo College of Foreign Languages, having majored in German. Captured in Manchuria by the Soviet Army, he was put into a concentration camp in Siberia for eight years. He was awarded the Mr. H. Prize. The *Return of Sancho Panza* was published in 1964.

BEASTS IN SIBERIA

that day
it became clear
under the sky
which never gets enough sleep
the fig ripened alone
i became myself
that day
alloying sand and iron

as if about to grate
somewhere in our bodies
a crevice sliced through
undoubtedly this was
a crevice a loud weeping
we dropped our axes at once
and turned our backs
to that homesickness
we promised to tend
like prayer

that day we knew
we were abandoned
as if we hung
at the end of a rope
slipped over the edge of the world
we muttered perfect words
which shall never be
meaningful to anyone else:

—remember beasts in siberia have
furry armpits in four corners!

Nagatomo

THE WIND AND THE MARRIAGE

although we came back from the tableland
to our summer
death continues
to think of us
we were free in the wind
but the ceremony still visits us
we must not forget
we were at some place
solemn
before a window of luminous rites
a tree agonized in the wind
a dog was beaten in the street
the wind should listen to the future
directly beneath
the ancient clock tower
we will turn onto the street noisily

Ishihara • 27

we will become the fragrance
abruptly
of our dark future

Nagatomo

FUNERAL TRAIN

No one remembers
The name of the last station
The train keeps moving
Through a foreign country
Where it is broad daylight to the right
And midnight on the left
Whenever it pulls into a station
A red lamp gazes into the window
The hard black lumps
Artificial legs and worn shoes
All are thrown in
All of them are alive
While the train is moving
Everybody is alive
Though the train smells of the dead
Surely I must be on board
Everyone is already half ghost
They lean against each other
They nestle against each other
They eat and drink a little
They don't need much
Some are fading away
On their already transparent buttocks

Surely I'm there
Leaning moodily on the window
Now and then
One of us bites
Into a rotten apple
Either me or my ghost
Unendingly
We overlap with our own ghosts
And separate from them
We wait for the train to arrive
In the far unbearable future
Who's driving this locomotive
Whenever the train crosses a gigantic
Black iron bridge
The girders thunder
Many ghosts
Suddenly stop chewing
They are trying to remember
The last station's name

Nagatomo

THE GREETING OF THE TREE

one day
a tree greeted
yet
it did not bow
rather
one day
the tree was standing
which is his way of greeting
and
when the tree is finally
a tree by itself
the tree is greeting
therefore the tree
though it died long ago
is greeting

Nagatomo

THOUGH DEMETRIARDE DIED
—at the prison of Baikal in 1950

though Demetriarde died
five men witnessed it
five men of different nationalities
on their faces a forbidden expression
which looks the same in Armenia
in Japan and even in Poland—
they survived!

the resiliently thick chest
which would repulse such cheap thrills
would no longer have been yours or mine

a red pine distinguishedly meticulous
and stubborn at Baikal
was not necessary to crush that man

—tracking him so closely
with such a dogged patience
upon turning around
he was caught in a strange trap
undoubtedly set by someone
a rope dangling
from the freezing white sky
powerfully jerked him away
with a wrenching of the earth

Demetriarde sunk into the ground
4000 kilometers from Moscow
—in the final winter of the five year plan

do you remember—that man
De-me-tri-ar-de
his name
was not the only reason
for his liquidation

originally he was one
of those old imperial guards
laughably commonplace in Rumania
even with a mustache
he was not yet convinced
of the orders

the spotted tundra filled
with spit and foot prints
twisted him
and his toe dug honestly
into the soil
as his shoulders and forehead
rose into the air
—his insides were torn apart.

though Demetriarde died
his death will make no difference
in a blind country that knows
only the red of the pepper

the sorrow that strangles the naked wind
with both hands
does not matter
to anyone
under the white and frozen
sound of a gun
fired into the sky
with a quiet and poor gun boy's
honesty
finally we put on our mittens
so that the number of fingers
will never be counted again
we put on our hats
so that the number of hairs
will never be counted again

Nagatomo

ANZAI HITOSHI 1919–

Born in Fukuoka Prefecture, Southern Japan. He was a reporter for the Ashahi Press, but now works for an advertising company. He published *My Notes on the History of Japanese Poetry*, and edited *Post-War Poetry* and *Songs of Love*. He published *Flower Shop* in 1955.

BLINDED CITY

It's like a photo of Picasso when he was old,
Sucking tongue-halibut bones,
From whose wrinkled profile
Jut thick bald eyeballs.

Before I knew it
This poster was stripped
From hotel-subway
And wet street walls.

Those eyeballs; where have they gone?
Those softly burning bison-like eyeballs:
When were they ripped
From this zinc-roofed capital city sky?

There's the blue skull of Nikolai Cathedral.
The stinking river runs like a soul.
Only the eyeballs are missing,
And people comb their tree-leaved hair
Incessantly with a blind man's hands.

Atsumi

SUNFLOWER

On the edge of a country road
I happened to meet
Van Gogh
Stupefied, standing hatless
In the sun's hot light.

Ah! A stream of blue sky
Over a deserted Dutch village!
But it's not just that. Everything
Becomes clearer
Only when I stand beside
This one flower.

Atsumi

SUMMER, 1945

I was sick that summer
The nation's peril increased each day;
Even to hear the tree's smell
Was luxurious to me.

Atsumi

TRAP

While the sun shone, soaked with falling rain,
a fawn passed in secret;
In the distance, with one sad cry, the form vanished:
an autumn rainbow like a deadfall in heaven.

Bean

LIKE A SIGNAL

From where——to where?
A road pierces the night's dark loneliness.

The last train, snow crusted,
Goes by crying like a heavy bird.

Under its shadow wings myriad faces flicker;
For a moment, I see all of them.

My arms clang down in relief;
Excitedly, my eyes change color to meet another loneliness.

I know only a few simple words.
I stand with my feet slightly lit by their radiance.

Atsumi

NIGHT SHOWER

O lonely Tokyo,
Zinc-roofed capital!

There's no Jacques Prévèrt here, but I
Will fill with tears the neon eyelashes
On that slender advertising pylon
Above police headquaters.
                              I will
Make a pool at the edge of the land-fill
And let the polio'd crabs play.
                        I will wash the coin
Lost in a dark alley. I will
Go downtown to douse a fire
Before the fire-brigade arrives.

Atsumi

OVERCOAT

Even after the light's turned off
We hear the sounds of the sea;
Even after the window's shut
Snow piles up on the roof.

And tempting me towards
The darkest corner of my mind
Your hair embraces me
Like an overcoat.

Atsumi

HOMEWORK

I memorize French declensions until midnight.
I wonder, what's the name of that insect?
Shouldn't I be able to remember easily?
Half of my life—blank spaces in this homework.

Bean

JEALOUSY

He started singing in a drunken way,
    "She'd even pour water on a drowning man,
      she was an evil woman . . ."
It was a blues song that went like that.

Adding my voice to his chocolate-colored bass,
several times I felt I was about to bring the wine
and hors d'oeuvres up out of my stomach.
I became disgusted with my own slippery sense
of racial equality.

Even at that he shook my hand
before leaving.
And no matter how I look at it
his hands were too fat.
The back of his hands and the palms of his hands—
disturbingly different colors.
And his heart and face were reversed in exactly
the same way.

After he'd turned off into the darkness beneath
the neon towers
I recalled. That young poetess I know.
Since she'd been having an affair with some Negro
her poems published in those skimpy magazines
had improved to where you had to gasp.

I was secretly jealous!
That is, even if I slept with a black woman or a
white woman
my poetry would probably not get better or worse.
But that young female poet sleeps with a Negro
I find that like a round fat pole my own sex
is hateful.

Campbell

IN THE MORNING, THE TELEPHONE RINGS

About the time I start the washing machine
the telephone rings.
He is but half awake; night still clings to him from the
waist down.

In the background a sound like a distant factory
as he pushes an electric razor across his face.
"Slept soundly and alone in my apartment," he says . . .
"Going to eat the ham and eggs you left."
If so then who is that with you there
facing the wall, her back to you
as she pulls on her brassiere . . .
If he had but not called
his lie would not have been revealed.
But mornings when the phone does not ring
a broken washing machine is what I am.
I can be proud—I'm a hard worker
and every day assiduously I yesterday renew.
I like the yard when blue sky spreads out over it,
particularly when the winds practically blow the children
to school.

With a grimace my husband fastens his stiff collar
just before it's time to board the bus.
And my lover every 20 days or two weeks
takes me off to some lonely town
there to thrust his fingers into my ears or mouth or
anywhere . . .
He can turn me gently inside out.

Campbell

Anzai • 39

A NEW RAZOR

my son uses the new razor clumsily
because this is the first time
to disguise himself as an adult
he is squaring his elbows
this is his ceremony
he is so intense
he will not shift his gaze
he's a little surprised
as a spot of blood reappears
like a bird's tongue on his temple
even as he wipes it off
inside him, what is bleeding?
his naked back
is wet and dazzling
as a tree trunk stripped of its bark
it seems that my son doesn't hear it
but birds are warbling
around the young tree trunk
it seems that my son doesn't see it
but a tide has moved in
in the mirror

Ayusawa

SO SAKON 1919–

Born in Kitakyusyu City. He graduated from Tokyo University, with a major in philosophy, and writes art criticism and fiction. He published the essays, *The Condition of Art*. *Kappa* was published in 1964.

DEDICATION
(from the verse sequence *Mother in Flames*)

Mother,
this volume is for you.
Twenty-two years after
you turned to flames
I have made it of paper
(that readily turns to flames as well)
to be your tomb.
In addition
it is my tomb too.
It is a tomb
where I am buried.
Even as I live
for you, burning endlessly,
and for me,
it is a common tomb,
Mother.

Herring

THE DEMON

Mother,
That night, you kindly turned yourself to roasted corn for my sake,
And therefore, each night now, twenty-two years later,
I take you out of the freezer that I made myself,
Apply my yellow teeth to your broken kernel rows
And chew.
The grains are scorched black, and taste bitter; even so,
Sometimes, when I happen upon one of the softer places
A sweetish syrup oozes out, and that is why
My teeth pull loose and stick there where I bite.
By this time, all my front teeth have got themselves transplanted
Wrong side up.
The corn looks like an epileptic hedgehog but
Somehow my canine teeth at least
Are with me yet. They've grown
And lengthened into fangs.
With these, I clench the corn firmly,
In my mouth, from left to right.
I use it as a harmonica, to play
Sweet sentimental melodies of childhood to myself
Each night now,
Mother.

Herring

EPITAPH FOR A KAPPA

Its eyes
Circle the heavens, greedily fixed on the beasts of burden
                                        of the slaves of life
Its bill
Rends the heavens, sniffing for death in the midst of life
Its shell,
Rising from rank mud, reflects the moon's rays upward
Its claws,
Amid the water-force of life, squeeze death's flowers open
                                        in widening wave-rings
Its eyes   its bill   its shell   its claws
Have decomposed; they are gone from here
Kappa—
You, who do not rest here—
By peeling you apart, layer after layer, egg-like
And rearing the embryo from within you
Dead as it is, to maturity here,
Until the day when this can be
The invisible tomb
Of the Kappa
Here
Plays will-o'-the wisp

Herring

When you were not looking, I
Thrust my soft hand through your posterior
And regaled myself upon your liver lights and lungs. Thank you.
I enjoyed the feast. By way of return
I have left my electric torch
There, inside your abdomen.
What will it illuminate within you?
I wonder.
Since, of course, it runs by battery
Sooner or later, it will burn out.
In other words, what I would say is this:
The electric torch—
Happens to be my tomb.

Herring

TAKIGUCHI MASAKO 1919–

Born in Seoul, Korea. She graduated
from the first Girls High School in Seoul,
and works in the Library of Congress in
Tokyo. She was awarded the Murou Saisei
Prize. *Iron Legs* was published in 1960.

ON MAN

He knows
between a woman's well-turned legs
a flower
blooms differently
in Spring
Summer
Autumn
Winter.
He speaks frankly
like a clairvoyant.
His robust voice
makes her blush
to the top of her head.

He wishes
his lover would die as quickly as possible
to make sure
she belongs to him.
On a winter day with a beautiful sky
he comes from behind
saying, "Die soon.
I'll carry your coffin."

He is in a hurry
to redden a green apricot,
to force open a rose bud.
He believes
a woman will ripen and fall
if he touches her with his palm,
as if he were Jehovah.
His palm is always damp with grease.

Kijima

FUTURE

A June night drenches bare feet in dew:
the young lovers first embrace.

To love is to grow heavy.
Words drip down from the dead.

Everywhere, stark white flowers
smother fields in the night.

The couple walks through
fields swarming with blossoms.

Heavens of night fall
on each fresh kiss.

A dead man's words can be heard through the twilight:
The future is farther than the distance you have come.

Kijima

BLUE HORSE

Sunken murmurs come from the bottom of the sea.
A horse, blind in both eyes, can be seen
through a crease of water.
The blue horse plods along the sea bottom;
the memory of a man on its back almost entirely gone.
How long has this horse lived in the sea?
Is the blood splashed on its back its own?
One leg brushes aside clinging seaweed,
and the horse's blind eyes become
a far deeper and lonelier indigo than the sea.
It moves unpretentiously on.
Blood oozing from its wounded belly
is washed off by sea-water
and carried from wave to wave . . .

A cold fog rises from the sea in autumn—
by a rock at the sea bottom,
the horse crouches alone, legs folded,
enduring the cold;
enduring the wait.

Kijima

JUST ONE

A pale, dirty face
drifts through lonely two a.m.;
carrying many bundles
I leave for dawn
a hundred zeros in the future,

Takiguchi • 47

for the certain place bright tides shine,
and someone has arranged clear lungs
and a perfect skull.
I show everyone waiting
a magic lantern slide of joy pressed over sadness;
and plants spill seeds endlessly,
and one warm ankle touches another,
and when just one life
begins to shine with silver light,
I shall return
remembering that a hundred zeros in the past,
someone on a staircase
watched me carefully.

Bean

FLAME

Two transparent butterflies fly
over the road no one has taken,
in the hour no one has lived.
Beneath street lights in strips of lamplight
they go quietly, side by side;
sometimes violently intertwining.

Then, one,
in order to die, takes flight
toward the enormous flame that makes the sky gleam.

Kobayashi

NAKAGIRI MASAO 1919–

Born in Kurashiki City, Okayama Prefecture. He lived in Kobe for 20 years; graduated from Nihon University, the faculty of Arts and Literature; and for twenty-six years was a reporter for the Yomiuri Press. He was awarded the Takamura Kotaro Prize. He translated the poems of W. H. Auden and C. D. Lewis; and was a member of the poetry group "Arechi" (The Waste Land). *Poems of Nakagiri Masao* was published in 1964.

SEVENTY NONSENSICAL LINES

My words are wrong
the monster's are strong
fear of torture (someone said)
all the women I have held
are like onions washed ashore
is there nowhere a woman real
sure as a Parker that never
needs shaking
my words sound wrong
the monster's are strong
wipe away thought and think
wipe away feelings and feel
listen all you like to the radio
weather reports international news
you can know nothing
cannot even be sure you are living

all seasons are the same
know the single unique thing (he said)
my words are wrong
the monster's are strong
where's the enemy where the traitor
nearest you you yourself
I know that
so is there anything you don't know
I know it all but not
how to say it
sinister laugh of a blackbird (hear?)
my words sound wrong
the monster's are strong
seek in a word no single meaning
in a rose no rosy colour
somebody grew a blue rose once
don't get mired in words
feed cats words fattened on mice
kiss dust that you may hope
but I doubt it (said someone)
things I say wrong
the monster speaks strong
Mohenjo daro Mohenjo daro
from the groin of a nude standing on her head
grows a tree
a man weighs dates on a scale
name of a city on the Indus
four thousand years ago
meaning Hill of the Dead
and kept on dying until just now
fitting name
my image for a civilization

tall tree falling toward dawn
what I say is wrong
the monster is strong
chasing time
's to be chased by time
never an excuse when late for work
prize the peaceful lonely heart
as if alone on a boat at sea
possible to be many and one at once
harvest and famine in the same moment
the things I say are wrong all wrong
the monster the monster is strong
water wanders among wines
light flows thinly on a frozen field stops
magnetic field enigmatic field
chunk of charcoal from which these my eyes
when will it burn all burn out
who yes who
will be responsible for 2 billion people
the monster comes quietly
Clyton why do you worry so
about what they'll all say

Fitzsimmons

A POEM FOR NEW YEAR'S EVE

The last night
The dark hours heading for the first day
The night to be with silently falling snow
With distant animals

The night being formed
In indefinable things
In every cold pitiful thing

A small unhappiness raps on the windowpane
The human eyes gleam with the sorrow of ash
The last song covers the earth
The sacred moment draws nearer
Gradually through the dark
That moment when death and life merge
Before the tiny spot in Time assaults us
Is there anything left for us to do?

At that sacred moment
We'll be informed
that all great words have already been said
That the promises of life are variations
                    of promises of death
At that sacred moment
All futures will flow through the door
                    opened for tomorrow
And the room will shine with lights of crystal and dark
At that sacred moment
I'll forget and will be forgotten
Like a corpse falling into the grave
I'll fall into my self
Into my narrow deep channel
Into my dark tomorrow

Sato

SPRING PILGRIMAGE

Like chains clanking somewhere,
he remembers several crimes on the spring beach at midday,
the penny he stole from a blind beggar,
didn't return but spent, the boy's shame,
I always crouch to fool the enemy,
patience, a while longer, till a day of triumph,
spine, don't get nervous, he told himself,
but I've been a hunchback to power all along, he realized,
the helplessness of that moment, the disgust.
Memory is a demon's ambush,
it assaults like a fever and routs the troops,
but why doesn't it open to the future,
whatever one has obtained torments one,
the subtlety of the prescription cannot be understood.
He raised his head and looked at the misty horizon,
but no hell is crueler than the collapse of a big dream,
no one mouths the terror of it,
because just mouthing it, its ghost tortures him,
if before I show what I can do
I get trampled down by death by the roadside
in a country with no relatives to claim me,
then, who can I hate, who can I appeal to?
A chicken, its anus swollen bare,
after tottering about,
gets smashed by a treacherous hand,
if that's the end of my world,
what kind of screech will I make at my last moment?
It can't go on like this,
no, it can't go on like this,

the shadow of the large hand looms dark over the
                clouded sky!
Among the rape plants where I slept with a white
                butterfly last night,
I writhed in sweat all night,
in the space like a ballot that I peered at from
                dream's solitary cell,
yellow pine pollen was falling vertically.
The day before yesterday, the day before that,
days I dip a spoon in the soup and scoop nothing,
the spring makes me forget my home and mission.
Home! It was also in the cruelest month,
I took off my clothes in a beach cave with shining cobwebs,
swam a while in falling rain,
and was proud, alone, with no one to tell . . .
(A woman laughs)
Now distant from it, on the beach of a strange country, I see
an ibis-colored camellia blossom swaying on ripples
                like bamboo leaves,
its shape, swaying but unmoving, denies all metaphors,
and is simply there, for that person.
He drooped his head,
yes I know, that's death's last warning,
"Dig your grave with care,
there's no time for grudging" . . .
He raises his head, turns toward his home,
yes, that's my mission, our mission!
First, physically train yourself,
when adult, learn eloquence, troop deployment, and finance,
to save your people with courage and virtue,
(A woman laughs)

what would happen to this mission, this big dream,
is this temporary collapse, or eternal impossibility?

I'd never ask you to remember us forever,
a man needs a broom of oblivion to live,
so if my book finds itself on the floor of a second-
              hand bookstore,
spitting black phlegm, it shouldn't complain,
only, remember us on occasion,
when we were shrunken like fetuses
and were flowing in the amniotic sea, we still knew
what the colors of shrine forests and streetcars were like,
even when all of us turned into a glob of strawberry
              jam, we still felt
a firm core at its center,
but now, we don't have hands to take up guns and flags,
we don't have tongues, lips, throats,
so we can't convey to the survivors
what we forgot to say (whatever that was),
charcoal powder broken into particles smaller than sand
exposed to sun, moon, and water until it became white,
remember on occasion the charcoal powder, which was
              weak-minded,
remember it and weep as you move chopsticks to your mouth.

Am I a temporary employee of life willing to be listed
              among failures,
or an eagle on a crag, staring at infinity?

Sato

ISHIGAKI RIN 1920–

Born in Tokyo. Since 1934 she has been working in Nihon Kogyo Bank. *A pan, an iron pot, and a burning fire before me* was published in 1959.

TRAGEDY

A hearse came along the Keihin Route
from the direction in which I was walking.

And,
in the driver's seat and assistant's seat
two men were laughing.
While talking about something or other.
In the assistant's seat the big fellow with the red face,
really seemed quite happy . . .
Ha, ha, haaaa . . . It seemed you could hear his voice
in his expression.
Laughing.

Quietly the hearse
passed my side
there was one coffin in the rear
passenger without complaint.

Then came three different colored taxis
filled with relatives in mourning clothes.
Riding sadly, downcast . . .
In that brief second
the funeral procession gently passed me.

"NO!"
Without thinking I turned, raised my hand and shouted.
As though giving directions to actors,
"Let's do it again,
from the beginning . . .
Have to start again . . ."

In the middle of the wide road it was.

Campbell

NURSERY RHYME

Daddy is dead
Put a white napkin on his head

Just as you cover
The food

Everyone cries
It's his unbearable taste perhaps

When mummy dies
I'll put a white napkin on her head
It's like the proverbial
Three meals

And when I die
I'll die like an expert
Like good food
Under a white napkin

Fish, chicken and cows
They die so well, so deliciously

Kijima

COCOON

It isn't that the threat of the bomb is great
but that the earth is small.

The silkworm eats
the mulberry leaves,
someone feeds on the world.
Who is gaining weight—a country or an ism?
(Anyway, not one of us.)

Look
something like thread
goes up in the air
something like smoke from a volcano
solidly surrounds the earth
and by the time it becomes a perfect cocoon
the chrysalis inside is killed.
What's left is an inch of silk.

Ayusawa

NAMEPLATE

You should put the nameplate
on the door.

The nameplate someone else puts up
brings no good.

When I was hospitalized
the nameplate said
Ms. Ishigaki Rin.

If you stay at an inn
you won't have a nameplate
but someday if you go to the crematory
the plate will be hung
on the closed door.
It will say
Ishigaki Rin, Esq.
Can I then refuse it?

Neither Ms.
nor Esq.
should be used.

You should put up the nameplate yourself
on the door.

Where the spirit lives
the nameplate shouldn't be hung by others,
Ishigaki Rin
that will do.

Ayusawa

AYUKAWA NOBUO 1920–

Born in Tokyo. He attended Waseda University, where he majored in English literature. After he returned from the war as a wounded soldier, he founded the poetry group, "Arechi" (The Waste Land). He published *Essays on Poetry* and *Notes During the War* and translated T. S. Eliot's poems and essays. *Poems by Ayukawa Nobuo* was published in 1955.

WARTIME BUDDY

My God . . . it sure has been a long time.
I thought that it was all forgotten now . . .
Twenty years, huh?
You look at me as though you are seeing back that far.

Well, put her there.

So you're still kicking around then . . .
And what a cold hand.

I suppose you can remember then?
—The bloody straits of Johore—
—The scorched hills of Singapore—.

And you can still hear then, I suppose?
The echoes of destruction on destruction,
The song the cannon roars
Down from the naval station
At some hour of death?

You crick your neck pretending not to understand,
—Like all those little foxes who hide
Between the books, behind the keyholes.
You and I can only meet now in the past.
Is there still some secret there?

Line up under orders right away,
The black forest of bayonets all ranged in place;
Face the enemy: silently attack.
—One evening over, and you're
Dead.
Where did all that firmness go?
How did it die away,
That incarnation of innocence itself
—That you could follow clear to the horizon:
Glory for our country! Love to your fellow countrymen!

This morning too, when you brushed your teeth
In front of the faucet
There was red blood
Mixed in that toothpaste green
And you spat it out.
You respectfully tied your little necktie
And took your little body, warm still
From the end of sleep,
And had yourself packed
Into the streetcar,
Going reluctantly to work:
To get
Just a little something
You have to pull in
Just a little money

Today too
Day after tomorrow, too.

If there's anything to answer, then, answer.
You, with the guts of a trembling little bride.
You, my wartime buddy.

No matter how much we all lose
How little have you gained,
Huh?
No matter what the liberation
Gained from any enemy
What reparations did you pay?
Eyes, or ears, or hands and feet
Of the unlucky ones who sacrificed:
What did you do for them?

Yeah, my wartime buddy,
Why don't you speak up, just a little?
If you look straight this way, at me,
What is it
That you cannot see?
Everything will be just fine for the shrewd ones
Has really come to mean
Safety at any price and
A backing into indolence
Does everything you get depend upon
Some endless ability for compromise?

Fighting in the sordid realms of profit, loss,
All of you who mimic life so well
Cry in a single voice that
It's a terrible time.

With some dreary bar girl to talk to,
Water turns to wine,
And you grumble that
Desire will not grow more reckless.

Hiding in the trunk of a great tree,
Your sentimental brotherhood
With fawning heads all stuck together
Sleep
And propagate
(within the proper bounds)
And fill your stomachs
And happily dream of heaven
(within the proper limits).

Don't you count up the storms that come?

Fate will size you up in a single flash of light:
It's been a long time coming,
This end of the world.

See you around,
Friend.
This is the first time,
Really,
For us to part
And I want
No idle kiss

See you around.

Rimer

MORNING SONG ON A FLOATING HOTEL
TIED TO ITS MOORINGS

You wanted to go far away
Through the heavy rain
You wanted to go away from the pain-stricken city
And look for the guards of death
When I touched your wet shoulder
The city turned into a harbour
And the smell of raw fish came through the night
The ship's black shadow sat on the wharf
The portholes lit up like nostalgic souls
Let's take a long voyage, I thought
And shake off this remorse
You thrown over my shoulders like a gunny sack
The telegraph wires humming in my ears

At dawn our fast ship
Might have carried our fate
Across the blue sea
We never got anywhere
Through the window of the shabby hotel
I spat on the city's early light
My tired eyelids, ash-colored walls
Our small hope caught in a vase
The wharf's crooked edge
Dissolved in stale water
I couldn't sleep all night
The odour of medicines stagnated in the air
It kept on raining
In the sad and empty valley
Between our separated hearts
And our burnt bodies

Did we strangle God in our bed?
We think of each other's responsibility
I put on my dirty tie
An invalid with peptic ulcers
You carry above your catlike shoulders
A tiny face
Made up like a vulture's
We sit down for breakfast
You smile, seeing in the cracked eggs
A half-ripened future
Your smile is a stupid smile
I stab my fork maliciously
And pretend I've relished
The oily dish of upper-class adultery

The landscape outside
Is inlaid in the window
Ah I want rain, streets and night
How else can I embrace this city of ennui
Born between the two wars
A failure at love and revolution
I threw out of the window
The ideologist's vagrant grimace
The city is dead
The fresh morning breeze is a cold razor
Touching the sores on my neck
A man's shadow falls on the canal
A wolf appears, its heart gouged out,
It cannot howl for ever

Yamazaki

IN SAIGON

There was no one on the pier
to welcome our ship.
A French town I had dreamed of
floated on the sea of an unknown colony in the Orient
and the body of a civilian employee
who had killed himself with a razor
was carried out of a hatch, wrapped in white cloth,
undulating.
That was our Saigon.
The sufferings of France
were the sufferings of her people
but were our agonies
the agonies of our fatherland?
Over a huge ship carrying a tricolor flag
was the clear blue sky
of a defeated nation.
When many friends die
and many more friends keep dying
how beneath the skin of the living
black worms begin crawling—
the sick soldiers talked
with the voiceless new dead.
In the bright wind,
the razorblade that liberated the young soul
laid on our thin throats,
the boat with the stretcher
slowly left, plowing the green waves.

Sato

THE END OF THE NIGHT

1

You frighten me; you,
like the night beach,
hold close the flow of my blood;
you frighten me; you
hook me onto love's sharp stake,
make my body writhe like a waterweed,
and tear it to shreds.
You frighten me; you
mouth vile prayers
and keep fondling my breasts,
a virgin who died by water.
I put my face, averted,
on the water of sorrow
and gaze into each one of
the distant stars, near stars—
Gentle one,
you cannot hold in your arms
the flowing river forever.
No matter how you love my black hair,
from the water's edge
where we meet, skin to skin,
my senses come off and drop
beyond the grasp of your fingers.

2

The bars confining us
are made neither of iron nor of wood
but of raw muscles;
I cannot escape these mobile bars,
however I try.

Your hot veins
entwining my thin neck
stifle the formless cry of my soul.
I don't know why I have fallen this far,
I don't know.
To us living in this windowless room
as if the day were the year,
the sun neither rises nor sets.
Where is our horizon?
My brain has only
a table turning round and round,
bits of bones and meat,
a grimy piece of cloth,
no love, no pity.
Again, I grope over the wall for the exit
and push open your breasts.

   3
  No one knows of our bedroom.
  The air pulls at the curtain.
  No one knows of our bedroom.
  The mist peers in from the ceiling.
Your hand is cold.
The five fingers are a weapon
like a poisonous snake.
What do you gain by killing me?
  Who is it
  playing the concertina of bones?

You are pale.
You want me to believe
you are not concerned any more.

What if I die?
   Who is that
   eyes full of blood?

Sato

BEYOND YOUR DEATH

   I
March 27, 1947
The unforgettable sorrowful face
appears to my surviving mind.
You were beautiful, my sister.
Now you hide in the grave:
you spoon milk into your own thin throat.
You never tell me, but
is it fun, a hide and seek of love and death?
I regret so much for
your breasts that never matured, for a pretty mole
on your cheek that never seduced a man.
The shadow of your childlike smile gently
caresses my soul brimming with desire.
My virgin sister,
are you really alone in the dark underground?
Why should I remember your breasts,
the pretty mole on your cheek?
Before your future ring collected blue light,
before the pendulum of your future clock begins to swing,
my sister, why did you take leave of life, in
your sweet baby talk.
I wipe fatigue off my glasses.

I dream of a deserted room.
My sister,
I lose this bet on life,
living with hunger, greed, a mean face.
Failing to be dead, what should I do with
tomorrow's setting sun in my back?

II
January 3, 1950
Wrapped in a mysterious night
where one year ends and another starts,
my soul is ill.
The blood fallen from
the evening sun
rots in my chest.
A lonely dream of flying
supports my falling body.
My sister, dead for 20 years, you still wander in the air.

Nobody sees you,
the darkness is fathomless.
My sister, a messenger from the world of death,
do you break the laws
that separate us?
You remove your full white death robe,
you come near my bed,
over me you throw the moist smell of ashes.
"If there are any laws that do not
belong to body or soul
our intercourse does not need
soul or body."
Your tapered fingers
fumble through my hair.

I tremble with an unearthly cold joy.
Nobody sees us,
the darkness is fathomless.
My sister,
let us go together leaving all hopes.
You can simply run away with your mischievous eyes and smiles.
I will keep chasing you, as a young boy years ago.
I couldn't love you fully,
I couldn't die completely, so
my sister,
let us be a pair of ghosts.
Let us run around in a dream
with no beginning and no end.

III

April 1952
A sheep away from his flock
shakes his milk jug in the clear air.
You are looking at him from behind the dark grove.
I lie on this little hillside, facing the shining sea,
I feel my aimless road ends here.
The green will of things under the sun
does not stay stained with regret.
It germinates like April's sprouts among dry leaves.
You are listening, quietly, behind the dark grove.
The sound of brooks hurrying to the ocean,
the songs of gulls returning to the cliffs:
they wipe away our injured memory.
Here, even the stones slowly
move toward the sea.
The mother sea and the sun keep me
from giving up my life.

I feel like building a house in this fragrant breeze
to live with my wife and some cattle.
You close your eyes behind the dark grove.
You will pretend to be dead forever.

Lento

WHY DID MY HAND

Why did my hand
reach your shoulder
with so much sinister gentleness
as if one of us was about to die

How could my smile stop your
tears. We have many other tears,
neither yours nor mine.

Do not say a thing
except to weep for the brevity of your long voyage
even if you had more to say.

In my hand's sinister
gentleness on your shoulders
the bone, flesh, and flower of blood
disappear like an aimless scribble.

Though I am holding it to myself
I could cry
because you, so pale, became thinner than
any regret

Lento

ODE ON WAVES, CLOUDS, AND A GIRL

June is a blue eye.
July is a fish swimming in the sky.
August is a white grave on the beach.
From this bright window frame
he left with the unforgettable summer
for the eternal offshore.

The storm left the cliffs
broken.
Above the roofs a cloud appeared and melted again:
like an enchanted phantom
that appears and disappears,
it melted into the infinite sky.

A voiceless scream
opens its mouth at the sea and sky.
A bird falls down to the window at dusk.
Then silence begins to sing—
an agnostic prayer,
a mute girl.

Lento

SEKINE HIROSHI 1920–

Born in Tokyo. He worked in a cardboard factory, a hosiery factory, an electric appliance factory, and others, and became a reporter for some trade papers. He is now a free-lance writer. He founded the poetry group, "Retto" (Archipelago). He has published *Eyes of a Pilot, Down with Monopolizing Capitals, Set Fire to Tokyo University*, and *My Town, Shinjuku. Dead Rats* was published in 1957.

SQUID AND HANDKERCHIEF

I washed
a squid and a handkerchief.
I dried the handkerchief
and went to bed.
Morning . . .
the handkerchief that was
supposed to be dry
had turned into the squid.
Last night,
what was it I ate,
a squid?

I mentioned this
at the meeting.
A certain poet
put it like this:
He washed a squid
and a handkerchief.

He hung the handkerchief out,
dried it, and went to bed.
When he woke up
the handkerchief had
turned into the squid.
He fried the squid
and ate it.
This is the image of
our times.

Campbell

ONE'S FATE

i see that
after tomorrow between Shinjuku and Tsukijima
the tram car will be removed
those guys with the socialist flag
surrounding the ding dong tram car in question
on top of its roof, repeating
the loud chant

in front of a closed tavern
in the dimness
while chatting
with a woman, a palm reader

i've heard
a guy with long hair
like an American hippie
a Japanese girl, a street freak
passed by murmuring frivolously
"what's it for? Vietnam?"

what a thing to say
the safest vehicle in Tokyo
is disappearing
what will remain?
the traffic war—more dangerous than Vietnam
disgusted though i was
i learned a lesson
from the woman, the fortune teller
"even though one can predict for others,
it's hardest to see his own fate
and so
we can still make a living."

Nagatomo, Kijima

ENEMY

dad's looking for an enemy;
to hell with the refrigerator
and the laundry
no doubt long ago
i was fed up
with the television
o without an enemy to bite
i will suffocate

then mom plays enemy
but the usual illness
begins again
like an eel mom escapes
dad's arms
the air is his enemy
then

helpless as he is
dad goes into a woods of neon signs,
where there are drums
and wild animals howl
woh
woh
there are lots of buddies
—only the buddies are not
the necessary enemy
he's looking for

and after all he returns
speaking to himself
in a lion's tongue
which is happiness
out of weak logic
o what a pitiful dad
unable to find a window
caged-in still

Nagatomo, Kijima

IN FRONT OF A BANK

there is a fellow selling rabbits
a proviso, saying that they will
not grow any bigger
i wonder if it means they will die
like my deposit which does not grow

there is a fellow drawing portraits
i wonder if those allowing him to draw them
not too exactly
are people who want just once
to experience the feeling
of being president

there is a woman, a fortune teller
telling fortunes in front of a bank
this is a frivolous joke
for, come morning,
even with no selling
the earnings will·be brought in

there is a hippie
futen as japanese say
mite or louse though he is
upon the wall of imitation marble
unable to suck blood

an emergency bell on the door
shutters firmly closed
sneering at the nervous twitching
a movie theatre across the street
the gangster with an audacious air
has succeeded at once in robbing
a bank down to its last penny
in a western town

Nagatomo, Kijima

TAMURA RYUICHI 1923–

Born in Tokyo. He graduated from
Meiji University, having majored in liter-
ature; and was awarded the Takamura
Kotaro Prize. He was a member of The
University of Iowa International Writing
Program; he translated the detective
stories of Agatha Christie, Ellery Queen,
and others; and was a member of the
poetry group "Arechi" (The Waste Land).
Poems by Tamura Ryuichi was published in
1966.

THE MAN WHO SEES THE PHANTOM

1
A small bird falls from the sky.
For the single bird shot in nobody's presence
the field exists.

A scream is heard from a window.
For the single scream shot to death in an empty room
the world exists.

The sky is for a bird. A bird falls only from the sky.
The window is for a scream. A scream is heard only from the window.

I do not understand why it is so.
I only feel why it is so.

A bird falls, so there is height. There is something
closed since a scream is heard.

As a bird's body occupies the field,
death fills my mind.
As death dwells in my mind,
no one lives inside any window in the world.

2

At the beginning
I was looking out of a small window.
At four-thirty
a dog ran past.
A cold passion chased it.

(Where did the dog come from?
Where did the skinny dog run to,
the dog of our age?)
(What darkness chases you?
What desire makes you run?)

At two o'clock
a pear tree split.
An ant dragged his fellow's corpse.

(What we have seen so far
began at its end.)
(When we were born
we had been long dead.
When we hear a scream
silence prevails.)

At one-thirty
from an extreme height
a black bird fell.

(Whose is this yard?
Whose is this deserted
yard in the autumn sun?)
(You, high above like a hunting bird!
Whose is this yard?)

At twelve
I looked at the yard
like a man who is looking into the distance.

3

The sky is filled with the flotsam of our time.
Even a small bird
must go through our embittered heart
to return to its dark nest.

4

A voice has ceased. When
I heard it in a bird cage at dawn
I did not understand
what it was searching for.

An image has dissolved. When
I saw it in a life boat in the dusk,
I did not understand
what its shadow was born from.

When the voice flies out of the bird cage
and forms our sky,
when the shadow breaks the life boat
and forms our horizon

my thirst is at the middle of noon.

Lento

NU

Some rooms have no windows.
In your mind there is a window with no room.

    Among bees humming,
    the torn skin of mind and things,
    rain shining on a summer day,
    and the dead,

you pause silently.
If your missing heart screams inside the window
before things take shape

    my ears do not hear her voice.
    My eyes hear her voice.

Lento

FOUR THOUSAND DAYS AND NIGHTS

For the birth of one poem
we must kill
we must kill many
we must shoot, assassinate, poison many beloved.

Look,
simply because we wanted the trembling tongue of a small bird
from four thousand days and nights
we shot the silences of four thousand nights and
the backlight of four thousand days

Listen
simply because we wanted the tears of a starving child
in all the rainy cities, the smelting furnaces and
midsummer wharves and coal mines
we assassinated the love of four thousand days
and the pity of four thousand nights

Bear it in mind
because we wanted the fear of a stray dog
who sees what we cannot see,
who hears what we cannot hear
we poisoned the imagination of four thousand nights and
chilly memories of four thousand days.

To give birth to one poem
we must kill our beloved.
This is the only way to resurrect the dead,
the way we must take.

Lento

OCTOBER POEM

Crisis is my condition.
Beneath my smooth skin
violent emotions storm,
a fresh corpse is thrown onto
October's desolate shore.

> October is my Empire.
> My gentle hand rules what is being lost.
> My small eyes watch what is disappearing.
> My soft ears listen to the silence of the dying.

Tamura • 83

Terror is my condition.
In my abundant blood
time flows, murderous, and
a new hunger trembles
in the cold October sky.

October is my Empire.
My dead troops occupy all rainy cities.
My dead patrol planes circle above the missing hearts.
My dead populace signs for those to die.

Lento

NARROW LINE

You are always alone.
Your eyes never show tears.
They have a bitter glimmer.
I like that.

To your blind vision
the world is a barren hunting ground, and
you a winter's hunter,
forever stalking one heart.

You do not believe in words.
In your footprints that murdered every heart
I read a thirst for fear.
That is too much for me.

On the narrow line you walk along
a bloodsmell hovers even in the snow.
However far apart you may be
I can sense it.

You pull the trigger!
I die in the middle of a word.

Lento

HOSHINO'S HINT

"Why do birds sing"
At a Press Club Bar
Hoshino read me an American poem.
"Why do people walk. This is the next line."
We drank beer
ate cheeseburgers.
At a table in the corner a middle-aged
Englishman lit his pipe.
His wife was intent on a novel of God and the Devil.
After the twentieth of September the fall
takes over the night of this briefless age.
We walked, silent, along the narrow asphalt road.
We parted at Tokyo station.
"Why do birds sing"
I came to myself in the dark:
what fell from high above moved me.
Then I returned
to my dream, to my "next line."

Lento

ANGELS

Above us
angels shut off "time"
to bear silence.

My silence with my eyes open
in a third-class sleeper, the 8:30 Hokuto from Aomori.
Which angel has stopped "time" for me?

If I gathered
the millions of lonesome lights outside the train window
in the dark from Ishikari to Kanto plain
I could not see my angel's face.

Lento

ON MY WAY BACK

I should never have learned words.
It would be good
if I lived in the world
without words, the world
that defies meanings.

If a beautiful word took revenge on you
that would have nothing to do with me.
If you bled because of its quiet meanings
that would be nothing to me.

If we had no words in our world
I would simply see and leave
tears in your gentle eyes,
pain that falls from your silent tongue.

Do your tears have any core of meaning?
Does a drop of your blood carry
a trembling resonance of this world's sunsets?

I should never have learned words.
Because I learned Japanese and snatches of foreign tongues
I pause in your tears;
I return alone into your blood.

Lento

WORLD WITHOUT WORDS

1

The world without words is a sphere at noon
I am vertical
The world without words is poetry at noon
I cannot stay horizontal

2

I will discover the world without words
with words I will discover
a sphere at noon, poetry at noon
I am vertical
I cannot stay horizontal.

3

June midday
The sun was above my head
I was among many rocks
Then
the rocks were a corpse:
the lava corpse of

the energy of
volcanic explosion
Why at this moment
are all forms a corpse of energy?
Why at this moment
are all colors and rhythms the corpse of energy?
A bird,
for instance, an eagle
in its slow spiral
observes but does not criticize
Why at this moment does it simply observe the forms of energy?
Why at this moment
does it not criticize every color and rhythm?
The rocks were a corpse
I drank milk and
tore at bread like a grenadier

4

Oh
the incandescent flow that rejects fluidity
the ice cold flame
that was not formed by love and fear
the forms of dead energy

5

The bird's eyes are evil itself
He observes but does not criticize
The bird's tongue is evil itself
He swallows, but does not criticize

6

Look at the sharply split tongue of a crow
Look at the woodpecker's tongue: a heathen god's spear

Look at the snipe, a tongue like a graver
Look at the thrush's tongue, a flexible weapon

He observes, never criticizes
He swallows, never criticizes

7
I went down a path as cold as Pluto
I walked 13 kilometers to the shack
along the flow of lava
down the path of death and reproduction
the path of the longest ebbing tide I've ever seen
I am a grenadier
Or
I am a shipwrecked sailor
Or
I am a bird's eye
I am an owl's tongue

8
I observe with blind eyes
I fall with my sightless eyes open
I destroy the bark stretching out my tongue
I stick out my tongue, but not to caress love or justice
Burrs growing on my tongue are not for curing fear and hunger

9
The path of death and reproduction
is the path of small animals and insects:
bees swarm up with a rallying cry,
a thousand and ten thousand needles lie in wait;
the path with no criticism or anticriticism,
no meaning of meanings,
no criticism of criticisms;

the path without vain construction or petty hope;
the path where metaphors, symbols,
imaginations are nothing
Here is destruction and multiplication
Here are re-creation and fragments
There are fragments and fragments in fragments
There are pieces and pieces within pieces
There is the base pattern inside the enormous base
The path of simile in a chilly June
Air sacs branch from red lungs
The air sac like an icebag fills with air
to the core of the bone and
the bird flies
The bird flies inside the bird

    10
The bird's eyes are evil itself
The bird's tongue is evil itself
He destroys but never constructs
He reproduces, but does not create
He is a fragment, a fragment in a fragment
He has an air sac but no empty heart
His eyes and tongue are wholly evil
But he is not evil
Burn   bird
Burn bird   all you birds
Burn   bird   little animals   all you little animals
Burn   death and reproduction
Burn

    11
Down
a June as cold as Pluto

the path as cold as Pluto
the path of death and reproduction
I run
I drift
I fly

I am a grenadier,
but also the brave enemy
I am a wrecked sailor,
but also the ebbing tide
I am a bird
and also the blind hunter
I am the hunter
I am the enemy
I am the brave enemy

   12
I will
struggle to a shack at sunset
Stunted, scrawny shrubs will become a big forest;
my small dream will shut out the lava,
the sun and the ebbing tide
I will drink a glass of bitter water
slowly as if it were poison
I will close my eyes, and will open them again
I will cut my whiskey with water

   13
I will not return to the shack
I could not dilute the words with meanings
like whiskey with water

Lento

YOSHIMOTO TAKAAKI 1924–

Born in Tokyo. He graduated from Tokyo College of Technology, with a major in electrical chemistry, and has published *Logic of Lyrics*, and *What is the Beauty of Language?*, and other essays. He edits the private magazine, *Trial*, and his complete works are being published. He was a member of the poetry group "Arechi" (The Waste Land). *Poems by Yoshimoto Takaaki* was published in 1958.

STORY OF THE AUTUMN OF FIRE

Eugene, stranger to me,
Autumn is here, the dark landscape is blazing.
I have every reason to believe
That your beating heart is aware of that.
You with the eyes of the disabled
Are crossing the Eurasian civilization.
You with your gunstock on the ground
Are brought to a halt at every quarter.
You are one of the soldiers
That may be doomed to defeat.

How heavy your footsteps;
How cruel the landscape you carry along on your back;
It is not migrants that are crossing the sky:
It is not human beings alone that are walking the pavements.

Eugene, you cannot but witness every landscape
As the last man of the Land of Sodom,
Remember the miseries of the Land of Gomorrah,
Beget by your woman what your eyes have seen.

Your death is sure to bring you repose,
Yet it will wound me with its dark notification.
A notification is bound to be a boundless burden for its recipient.
Suppose I am walking
To get rid of the burden
By a dark canal or
In a backlane between unshapely buildings;
Suppose the time is autumn,
Autumn that has come to the dark blazing landscape;
Suppose I have lost every bit of love;
Even then have I to trudge on with each weary step?

Eugene, answer me,
Answer me before you meet with a cruel death in a desolate land.
The world will shortly be burned down and be silent
As a gambling house where foolish games are all finished.
You will die for a cause that you believe is absurd.
Your eyes will dry out on a tiny thorn.
Your eyes will go on rejecting the sun and the sunlight.
Your eyes will never fall to sleep.

Eugene, this is my story of the autumn of fire.

Yamada

SPLIT PERSONALITY

An uneasy season lapses into autumn,
And the other you within you never returns;
Quickly awake from your delusion;
You are still thinking you have lost your girl's love.

Oh your sense of loss
Is shared by the whole world.
Can you in your small arms embrace
Not your girl but a landscape immersed in shame?
Can you in one act of espousal grasp
The revolutions bursting like volcanoes all over the world
And the massive atmospheric pressures and temperatures over them?
The other you within you never returns.
"He" has run away from you
With your notebook of pseudo-pastorals with dates,
With girls' love and tenderness,
With the repose of sleep,
With the approbation of Order and God,
With the fun of cunning contrivances,
With the comfort with strings to it,
With almost all the memories of your past.

Your landscape, already strange to you, lapses into autumn;
In an obscene city at the limits of Asia
You are looking, as if at phantoms,
At almost all the flowers of shame
That bloom from girls' lust and
Walk the streets;
You know delusion and solitude falling on you as damage;
You sense funerals approaching from before and after;

You stroll in any metropolis of hatred
With the eyes of the disabled.
You need not believe the doctors
Who may tell you that you need
A little recovery and a little trust.
Your sense of loss
Is shared by the whole world.
Winter is nearing upon a vast human avalanche;
Your salvation and cure depend upon your checking it.

The other you within you never returns;
Do you believe that the bombardment's voltage will bring him back?
Oh you never will.
Your fall and your autism
Are shared by the whole world.
Uneasy birds are migrating over uneasy autumn.
Their silence reflects yours.
When they scatter into the grim skies,
Your mind too scatters into the grim future.
Wretched uneasy season!
This earth that you tread as an invalid
Is erecting at the limits of Asia
A prison and an asylum

Yamada

TACIT UNDERSTANDING

Your petty defeat,
By the morning's dim canal flowing with garbage,
Turned your heart to that of a wretched vagrant's,
Gulping, like a momentary muddy flood,
Your privation and your girl's betrayal.
That is all that has happened.
Yet you cannot help being wounded.
That makes you and your mornings the darker.
That is the possible source of your revolt.
That plants the seeds of desperation everywhere.
The bitterness you feel for human frailty
And for human beings is genuine.
Doubt and pain you feel because of the uncertainty
Of the root of all justice and revolt are genuine.
On this enormous stage of the earth,
Riches and security establish justice;
Small disgraces turn to big rebellion.
Each trick can be justified in its own way,
But the juggler can never be hurt by his trickery.

Never cease to think
That the grace of almost all justice
Has long been divorced from the postulate;
That, when you or I depart from happiness,
It also has a will to depart from you or me;
That the Absolute or God is nothing
But hocus-pocus substituting a moment for eternity;
And that the juggler's sorrow, despair, and avarice
Are supporting his trickery.
O That is why

Either you or I am one of those not very deft jugglers,
One of those mean pantomiming actors
Disclosing their own trickery.
Upon life's precipice is always waiting
In ambush that shady enigma.
Behind every landscape is hidden that ugly look
Of tacit understanding between human beings.
This morning while you are frustrated by your little defeat,
I am suffering a complex.
This is the season of our disgrace.

You who believe that no very sure cause can be found,
I who believe that no anguish worth while can be found:
We must in any case set off,
Getting out of our dark hunger and
Uniting our respective revolts.
You excrete your little defeat
Into women's fields, and then
Dandelions and violets burst, distorted
As if by your failure.
You have to cherish that spring in the nineteen-fifties.
I turn up every bit of tacit understanding;
I tear down everywhere that misty atmosphere
Muffling the lithosphere.

O Then almost without fail
A landscape is bared,
In which
You are raising a row of flowers of shame.

Yamada

Our flesh lost, only our will sustains us.
We emerge as ghosts from the November graveyard.
Silent are our skies far and wide.
Cruel our earth below far and wide.
O Our autumn, of which we are no more capable of singing.
O Our heart, which is changing its way of singing.
Only because we are alive, gloomy are our fellowmen.
Only because we are not dead, hopeless is our earth.
Only because we have lost reasons to be alive,
We are the bond uniting our fellowmen and their destiny.
When we lost our love, we lost our flesh.
When we felt kinsfolk-hatred,
Our fellowmen buried our flesh in the graveyard.

O A sheet of wind alone
Cloaks our flesh with clothes
Proper for the period between autumn and winter.
Our flesh commits incest with the wind.
As ghosts we emerge
From the graveyard where crows croak to each other.
Our clothes have been turned cruel.
Our landscape has been darkened.

One half of the shame lies here, brought forth from our soil;
The other half lies there, inherited from the Son of David.
We are compelled to drudge as in those ancient days.
We shelter rebels within us to break the chains.
Soon our skies will start speaking;
People beneath our skies will rise to conflict.
Our city stretches sheer to the beach,
Our industrial areas send forth soot and smoke onto the sea.

Our whole life has not changed us,
The sea remains the same in its hues, with its flotsam.
Our shame will ripen, burst, and wither,
And then we shall die on the sunny streets.

O Would our shame and our despair be unearthed
Out of the future boundless city and its industrial areas?
Then brightness would transmute human beings,
Our genes would forget our shame,
Our despair denied any meaning;
Because of the difference between rebellion and support
Our corpse would be scourged.

O Season, close to death again,
Our somatic will remains alive covered with dust.
Mute drudge is our punishment.
When the future state of affairs is utterly invisible,
Our labour is compulsory grave-digging.
No means we have, except our fatigue, to identify ourselves.
Cruelty is strained as our breathing.
The world confines us all over the earth.

Yamada

The domed sky is serene and clear.
Like buck-shot birds fall on me,
Turning into as many anxieties.
This tranquil sky I will disturb,
Turning myself into a rejected Thought.
Because they are destitute,
My countrymen will not accept me,
And they are accepting the disadvantageous distress with two arms.
If I pay a visit, they meet me, frightened
As if at a foreign, forbidden Thought.
Why should I unfold my Thoughts
Before them like some obscene picture?
My beloved countrymen with their heredity of wretched submission!
Treat me to at least a cup of powdered tea.
Let me produce some rice-crackers from my pocket.
And let us listen speechless
To all the sounds this uneasy autumn raises.
You hear over empty dishes and plates clatter;
I hear the massive earth roar
That still goes on turning.
Then let us say goodbye to each other;
For our terms have been kept safe.

And yet I am as good as refused at every home.
However firmly the distress of impending catastrophe unites us,
Our different interests can be the main cause of our break-up,
Uneasy autumn's draughts pass through my heart.
I earn my living with my body and arms.
The place that consumes my heart and body
Is the factory that produces the Establishment.

The direction of every wind and smoke
Seen from this place of labour
Invites me into an imcomprehensible anxiety.
From this place the human horizon cannot be seen.
Buildings and show-windows cannot be seen.
O Yet I am dreaming of nothing.

Workers who think of me as a familiar neighbour,
For you I have kinsfolk-hatred.
I am your enemy as much as I am the Establishment's.
Jeering at your struggle,
Wearily I roll a gasoline drum.
In your homes I am pinned down
As a specimen of an idiot.
Yet I cannot die in your specimen cases.
I stand my bitter isolation among you countrymen.
My beloved countrymen with your heredity of wretched submission!
It is no use trying to lure me into sleep
With your genial affection.
It is no use demanding of you the affirmative.
Turning myself into a rejected Thought,
I will be living for the sake of its meaning.
I am descending to the bottom of the dark stairs of the Establish-
    ment.
I am falling asleep where punishment ceases to dog,
For the foreboding of catastrophe is sure to come to wake me.

Yamada

YAMAMOTO TARO 1925–

Born in Tokyo. He graduated from Tokyo University, having majored in German literature. He writes art criticism, and has published the essays, *Poetry's Native Place*. He teaches German at Hosei University. *Walker's Praying Songs* was published in 1954.

HIROHITO, AN ELEGY

Hirohito looks rather sad.

In dense fog,
listening to a music box,
from behind
he looks like Buddha.
He must be sad.

Perhaps Hirohito's heart
is bound to a primitive man.
A primitive man
wraps his passion in fig leaves
and throws his melancholy into the dusk
like fireworks.
Exiled by monkeys,
primitive man's solitude,
flowing deep in valleys,
wells out of Hirohito's eyes.

Ah, now!
In the forest the monkey clan
thrives by its cunning.

Hirohito's throne drifts.
In the strange freshness of a flower garden;
muttering; and a milky fountain;
Hirohito understands birds' voices.

For that reason Hirohito
closely resembles a god
fondling the sorrow of the fable's motherland
with his toes.
He stares at the distant image of man.
Only monkeys will survive.

Does Hirohito break out of the garden
and steal a handful of rice?
Let's not pray for him anymore.

Let's stop calling him
to join the procession of monkeys
who walk in the mud,
cherishing a slight remorse.

Nagatomo, Kijima

A CONTRACT IN SUNLIGHT

Let's greet the sun.
Let's walk barefoot on the smashed earth.
I'm so in love with you
I piss to heaven.
It's wonderful! My cock's so heavy,
com'on, let's bury
shiny seeds
in the soft, deep soil.

Forests sparkle,
fields glisten.
Even if our violent embrace
binds our legs with heavy shackles,
we must do it for maturity.
But we should not take advantage
of our fair climate;
not overindulge.
Our careful experiments with love
rise in the boiling light.
Let's take off our crazy affected clothes.

Hurrah!
We'll make our contract right under the sun.

Nagatomo, Kijima

THE LAW

So . . .
there's no other way:
we must throw ourselves
into temptation.
Within reach of the enemy,
we'll stagger
in search
of their system;
suddenly attack at the throat . . .
If we don't discover the enemy's scheme
we must struggle
until we've got it.

Having baited the trap,
to catch nothing is to catch shame.
All rulers
rot from imperatives.
We lack words for possession.
Therefore, our right to live
grows.
Now,
we must change our plans.

Nagatomo, Kijima

SINCE I NURTURE LIES

Since I nurture lies in my heart,
I can easily see through my country's foil of peace.
Since many lies disciplined me,
I must strike back alone.

"People!" Don't call us that,
you chancellors.
"We!" Don't sing that in chorus,
you revolutionaries.
I am not only a prosecutor of the powerful.
Confronted by a world of assailants and victims
in conflict, I am also a man.

Nagatomo, Kijima

POSSESSION

Our words are charming.
"Flesh," once said;
we immediately cling to the earth.
"Spirit," if spoken;
we are already flying.

Our souls belong
to gravity and buoyancy,
to suspicion and aspiration.
The world is made of coercion,
causes, and mistakes,
but surely, a blue the same as the sky
hangs deep in our skulls.

Otherwise,
standing on fragile legs,
how could we ride the image of wings
to possess endlessly higher places?

Nagatomo, Kijima

IBARAGI NORIKO 1926–

Born in Osaka. She graduated from Toho College of Pharmacy. An originator of the poetry magazine, *Kai* (Oars), she has written some radio scripts, juvenile biographies, and folk tales, and has published four volumes of poetry. *Dialogue* was published in 1955.

SOUL

You sit valiantly; an Egyptian queen
in the innermost chamber of a cave.

From paying you tribute,
my legs are ignorant of rest.

To flatter you,
I stole a vain offering.

But I've never seen
your blue and dark eyes
smiling like lakes;
blooming like waterlilies.

Your skin
sits on an enormous chair,
a lion's head carved on it,
smelling of ebony.
Occasionally I raise my candle
and kneel at your feet.

You set free light from Sirius and wear it as a necklace.
You set free light from Sirius
never raising your eyes.
The maddeningly futile questions and answers,
and metaphysical drifting
begin again.

Sometimes,
I take up a mirror
and look at your slave.

I see
a young Japanese face,
waiting to discover itself,
frozen, and a fire deep within.

Kobayashi

THE INVISIBLE MAILMEN

1
In March peach trees bloom;
In May wisteria suddenly entangles itself with flowers;
In September grapes grow heavy on the trellis;
In November green oranges start ripening.

Underground, slow-witted mailmen,
caps pulled back, pedal bicycles
from root to root,
toting each season's transient spirit.

To the peach trees of the whole world,
to the lemon trees of the whole world,
to every plant they bring
stacks of letters, multitudinous orders.
But they get lost, especially in spring and autumn.

Perhaps that's why pea flowers open
and acorns drop
at different times north and south.

I picked figs one morning
as autumn slowly grew fuller,
and I could sense the veterans
scolding the absent-minded substitutes.

2

In March rice-crackers are cut for the Doll Festival;
In May Mayday's song runs the streets;
In September farmer's eyes rock between typhoons and rice paddies;
In November young men toast young women.

Above ground, there is a post office of non-nationality
whose invisible mailmen make their faithful rounds
bringing men the spirit of transient times.

To the windows of the whole world;
to the doors of the whole world;
and the nights and mornings of every race;
they bring multitudinous suggestions and multitudinous warnings
but the messages get lost in waste lands and in the aftermath of
     wars.

Perhaps that's why the renaissance flowers
and revolutions bear fruit
at different times north and south.

One morning an unknown year was just beginning.
I shut my eyes and saw
human flowers growing, feeding on nothing.

Kijima

MY CAMERA

My eye
is the lens

My wink,
the shutter

I have a tiny darkroom
surrounded by hair,

and that's why
I don't carry a camera

Do you know, I've many pictures
of you inside me?

Your laughing face in sun filtered through leaves,
your radiant, chestnut body crossing waves,

lighting a cigarette, in a child-like sleep,
smelling of orchids—in the woods where you were a lion

In the world, just one; a film library
nobody knows

Kobayashi

OUTRUN

When you feel you've outrun somebody,
without trying to,
or even knowing you were running;
you feel an indefinite loneliness.

One night I outran father,
and cried on a damp pillow without a sound
while he snored, one room over.

And I hate myself for it now.
Hate myself!
I'm not better than he is.

But I outran him,
and like a revelation,
or sword-slash,
it marks a phase of my life.

I wonder if I'll ever give
young friends, nieces, nephews
such a moment.

When you've outrun somebody, you know it.
But if you're outrun, who's to tell you?

Kobayashi

SUICIDE BY HANGING

My father, the town's only doctor,
was called to an inquest
by the police.

He didn't mind my going along
since in those days I had to see everything
for myself; even an amputation
without the least light-headedness.
When I described the operation to a young scholar I dated
he sneered, saying, "It sounds like butchery."
Because of that, I dropped him.

In pine woods by a beach
on the appropriate branch of an appropriate tree,
a victim of suicide hung, in torn army clothes,
swinging in the wind like a rag doll.
First he had tried to kill himself in the ocean,
his trousers still sticky with the tide.
There was some change in his pocket;
last night the town must have been full of lights,
but had he no place to go?
Did he die for some reason other than food or money?

I watched, shaking and curious.
At home mother threw salt at me furiously
screaming, "Such a girl to go to that place!"
Father, who finished the inquest, is dead now.
The past is a distant memory,
but the rag doll,
whose tight-necked figure embraced all the miseries of life,
still swings in my mind from time to time:
in the tenderness of people,
in their compassion.

Kobayashi

YOSHINO HIROSHI 1926–

Born in Sakata City, Northern Japan.
He graduated from Sakata Municipal
Commercial School, and was a member of
the poetry group, "Kai" (Oars). He is now
a free-lance writer. *Illusion Method* was
published in 1959.

TO MY FIRSTBORN

One day soon after you were born.

Like vultures
They arrived
Zipping their black briefcases
Open and shut

They were life insurance men.

(What quick ears they have!)
I showed my surprise
They replied, smiling,
"We got wind of it."

Where
In your soft body
With your features still hidden
Have I given you
A little share of death?

Already
Its fragrance drifts on the breeze
They said

Inoue

EVENING GLOW

As usual
The streetcar was full.
And as usual
A young man and a girl were seated,
While the old kept standing.
The girl, with her eyes lowered, stood up
Offering her seat to an old man.
In a hurry he took it,
And got off at the next stop without thanks.
The girl sat.
Another old man
Was pushed aside in front of her.
She lowered her eyes.
Yet again she stood up
And offered her seat
To the man.
He got off at the next stop, thanking her.
The girl sat.
As the proverb says, *never two without three*,
Still another old man
Was squeezed out
In front of her.
Poor girl, she
Lowered her eyes
And didn't stand up this time.
The next stop
And the stop after the next
She remained stiffly seated,
With her lips compressed—
I got off the streetcar.

How far she rode on, I wondered,
Growing rigid with her eyes lowered.
A kind person
Is always an unintentional sufferer,
Wherever it may be.
Because a kind person
Feels the pain of others
As if it were his own.
How far the girl could have gone
With that gracious heart torturing her, I wonder.
Biting her lips
With bitterness,
Without once looking up at the beautiful evening glow.

Inoue

A CHAPTER ON THE BREAST

Young girl—
However modest your attempt to be happy,
Your rich and round breast
Pale and tense
Swelling improperly upwards,
Looks almost sharpened
Through your gauzy summer dress.

Like the blind prow of a ship
Equipped beyond her capacity,
Your breast is shining,
And shapely enough to catch
A man filled with trembling.
Therefore, a man, deeply ashamed,

Pretends not to notice,
Fearing she might be a mere companion,
Like a jutting rock,
Like a sunken reef,
In the way of the ship.

All that he can teach a woman
Is that the rich fullness of a breast,
Unmanageable to man, disturbingly insistent,
enchants him.

Inoue

BEING STUDIED—AN EMBANKMENT SUGGESTED

I took part in the 33rd May Day Central Rally,
After long, tedious greetings,
After our feet got stiff,
At last, after noon,
We began to march in five directions.
Toward Shibuya,
I walked and sang with fellow workers.
—Why no zigzag parade?
—The traffic's too heavy.
Some voices of demonstrators.
I seemed to have heard those remarks
Somewhere before.
After coming home,
I reopened the morning paper
To make sure it had promised no zigzag parades.
Earlier this morning I'd glanced
Over the print of the paper

And it seemed to subtly control me.
Maybe traffic is really heavy
Or perhaps the May Day Committee themselves agreed
To do no snake dancing.
But I'm not sure,
It's just a guess,
my doubt remains.
That type face
Could have been an embankment of cunning suggestions.
The water of May, channelled by the embankment,
May have flowed obediently away, singing.
I fear
We are
Being studied
Thoroughly, in secret.

Inoue

TO MY WIFE

To be born
and to die
may be some remote revenge
upon a man
said Mr. Saga.

Therefore,
a man and a woman
must be a set of traps
which make the revenge eternal.

Yet I linger
in the tender awkwardness of my youth
I felt when I discovered
that my wife had this weight.

Perhaps
there also may have been a remote blessing
that originated outside of remote revenge.

Lying beside my sleeping wife,
I feel a little restless with the mysterious affection
which seems to have been entrusted to a woman's body
and which gives weight to a man's soul.

Kijima

PERFUME "GOOD LUCK"

To an American soldier
returning to Viet Nam—
from the T.V. screen
after his five-day leave in Japan,

"Good luck!"

wished the interviewer.

I'm twenty years old. No steady girl yet.
A smile touched
his tensed brows;
the Pfc.'s name was Clark.

And the interviewer said,
"Aren't you a little reluctant
to go back to the war zone?"

"Yes, but I control myself."

"But on what grounds then
can you manage to fight?"

"Well, to protect the freedom
of my country. Isn't that enough?"

Built small, keen eyed.

Soldier, duck in.
Death's coming to meet you in a straight, gleaming line.

Battles have taken extra pounds
of your already meager flesh,
extra fat and skepticism,
and made your muscles slender,
strong, supple.

That's the training of the field.

"Good luck!"
he said to your back as you returned to war!
It was like a small cry issuing from
a broken perfume bottle
dropped from some awkward hands trying to bless:

"Good luck!"

What terrible bits of life!
What smells of death!

As if dissolved
into the rising stench
he disappeared
behind a pale screen.

Kijima

KURODA KIO 1927–

Born in Yonezawa City, Northern Japan. He was a worker during World War II in Tokyo, and after the war participated in the movement for farmers' liberation in his native district. A member of the poetry group, "Retto" (Archipelago), he published the essays, *Hunger unto Death*. *Anxiety and Guerrilla* was published in 1959.

IMAGINARY GUERRILLA

Days and days of walking
a gun on my back
the road twisting
threading one strange village to another.
Beyond is a village I know well.
And to which I return.
Must return.
Eyes closed
it is there: shape of the forest
a path through fields
roofpeak
how to pickle vegetables
all the relatives
a scrap of farmland to haggle over
petty formalities and whitewashed walls
white always
a broken hoe and other people's soil
fathers and their fathers cringing into death

mothers driven off. . . .
I return.
On a secret path I remember well
I jump from ambush, rifle poised.
This is the season of revenge
keeping blood fresh in the old old wounds.
The village is beyond.
Here the road knits strangeness to strangeness
and I find nothing I know, as if in a dream,
alone on the road.
I ask the way to a house
and find silence:
walls with no windows
no doors.
Another house
no windows or doors.
No one.
No sound.
Now the road hides in a village the colour of . . . what?
Where am I?
Where does the road go?
Tell me, please.
Answer!
The gun in my hands again I face the silent houses.
But something is wrong . . .
the weight in my hands is wrong . . .
wood—a rod of wood three feet long.

Fitzsimmons

HUNGARIAN LAUGHTER

Believe me
I was hanged
head over heels
killed
in Budapest where entirely a stranger
I was

Hang them
enemies of the people
someone shaking me
someone hitting breaking my head
saying
He's still breathing
cruel
not knowing that at nine this morning
I was eating salt salmon

How can they understand groans
in Hungarian
groans of hatred
Have they seen stomachs bigger than bodies
eyes blind legs
that run before
belly hands that leave
shoulders to strangle

I see the streets of Budapest headlong
I am hanging upside down
free streets are over my head
burning streetcars under my nose
the incredible burning of myself

Incredible
Yesterday I was trying to make
the wife of a friend
'No.' she said and
I hurried home raging
to throw myself on the bed
but
believe me
hungry Hungarians attacked me
eaters of wheat bread
I eat rice
and I know hunger
hunger of love and
the real hunger
more bitter than love

Vision of famine all over the earth
of the cities' deadly opened mouths
seeing for a moment
among chimneys and derricks
and dogtoothed trees
famine run wild
I too am forever hungry and blind
able to run only with legs
scratch with loose hands
I shake the corpse
looking for a hate object
drunk with my own execution

Then a shell knocks down the clock tower
the hands fall fluttering to the snow
time has vanished in Budapest
and so has mine

of whom should I ask the time
I must by tomorrow write
a poem about Hungary
Who is Rakoshi
that one hanging
Where is Nagy
gone lost
as I am lost

Walking in the deep belly
of a gigantic factory
on the breast of a wonderful kolkhoz
drinking a glass of socialist Tokay
where is her house really
is she living with someone
pretty house in the country
give me her body
body not spoiled by anyone
her body
her belly and breasts
No
give me
the gigantic factory
the kolkhoz belonging to no one
the sweet Tokay
pour the soup in a vacant belly
hot Hungarian soup

The winter of 1956
snow in Budapest
footprints on the snow
a stray child creeps up the hill
singing the song of the Partisans

Here is my home
When I enter a strange face stares back at me
thin dead face asking
Who is it
Rolling out I turn back turn back
a crowd of people like a walking snowball
march of the homeless crowds
march of blindness irregular steps

Streets deserted
what flat is that
you always keep
in the deserted streets
comrades
what flag is that
you carry
A snow flag
snow-white flag
Are you against the revolution
No look
flapping over my head
flapping over my head
awful miracle
Horthy's flag
whiter than snow!

Street corners blocked
tanks coming up
among them a trumpet sings
a husky Rakoczi march
cry on a white horse

Cry
bronze statues

Budapest city of bronze statues
standing so long
now they lay down on the ground
bronze lips mumbling
the old things were easier
to understand
who are the enemies of the people now
what should we do
I tell you what
just turn the turret
aim
fire at the counter revolution

I hate all counter revolutionaries
I hit them
again again again
What happened to them
I don't know I'm gone
in Budapest where
entirely a stranger
I was

Believe me
wise comrades
it is strange
very strange
I laugh
my corpse laughs
trembling corpse
that can't do anything but laugh
In Hungary
laughter of the pungent Chaldash

Fitzsimmons

THE BREEDING OF POISONOUS WORMS

on the four and a half mats of the room
our only room our home
my mother starts fussing around
now that you've been able to get
a job I can raise silk worms
again after thirty years
chops up something green
into a basket it's a shame
we haven't got mulberry leaves
but I've saved the eggs
late autumn eggs from
the year you were born takes
a bunch of sandy nits from the old
trunk carefully puts them in the basket
then squats there in front of it
now that you've finally found a job
silk worms again think of it
for the first time in thirty years
in the morning leaving I look at them
grubby in the basket no change nothing
don't worry they'll hatch soon
and as I come in that night from work
almost it won't be long now so
I try to be nice sure mom they'll
hatch tomorrow try to sleep
now but she just sits watching
like she's set for the night I
sleep dream of an ochre lane
under a brutal midsummer sun
and two long rows of mulberry trees

burning wild dead worms
falling soft plopping on the road
under the flaring trees millions
millions and millions of worms
in the morning leaving I look no
change but now they smell stink
like they're beginning to rot but
you'll see today they'll hatch we'll
be busy better buy some mulberry
leaves on your way back some
where my feet stop and I lean
against some sooty tree on a grimy
Industrial Avenue what the hell's
going on seventy years old and
still obsessed with a handful
of land lost so long ago mulberry
growing land hers ours nothing
but a fantasy in a grey head old but
my fantasy new of tractors on the land
is it her head they need does my
dream need hers begin there no
matter tonight I'll make her
sleep tell her a story of a fine new
collective far away in Russia
and while she sleeps her dreams
I'll dump those illusion breeding
worms into the nearest canal
on the way home I get some greens
and when I reach the door I freeze
sure now that the damn things
have hatched are in there right now
eating my mother a soft slithering

munching tide of worms nibbling
at her swallowing digesting I
rush in she smiles see see
they're alive and brings the basket
already some have crawled out to
wriggle around on the mats
brown an inch long crawling
across the floor inchworms no
no same mud brown skin but
different antenna mutations maybe
of a thirty year obsession but they
look like those poisonous near-eastern
worms that feed on desert plants I
stiffen imagining the feel of them but
now I've got to tell her I choke
it out the revolution's dead here
mother revolutions are only for
far away places desert places and these
things aren't silkworms I've never seen
silkworms like these but as she
comes closer I can see worms in her
hair on her shoulders and she smiles
yes there's one on her face revolution
what revolution has your dream come
back don't worry chop some greens
you'll feel better I just stand there
no words already can feel them
crawling onto my bare toes but my legs
won't move and I take the green stuff
hands like claws and begin tearing it
                              tearing

Fitzsimmons

KIJIMA HAJIME 1928–

Born in Kyoto. He graduated from Tokyo University with a major in American literature. He wrote stories, novels, picture books, and an opera libretto, and translated Langston Hughes, Nat Hentoff, and others, and was a member of the poetry group, "Retto" (Archipelago). He teaches English at Hosei University. During 1972–73, he was a member of the University of Iowa International Writing Program. *My Searchlight* was published in 1971.

DREAM

My dream—
What a limitless carrying cloth!
Curtains always open;
a camera panning
in all directions.

In my dream
the natural and possible
crash into each other
with equal force
pierced by the fangs of the dead.

My dream—
Gambling without a chance of winning;
no method of defense,
always happy at the surprise attack;
brilliant incoherence.

In my dream
now the attack; Aa!
Galloping into a brain-cave,
feeling the dinosaur's skin,
the trembling slug.

My dream—
What an incredible affection for yarns.
The feeling of everything pressing my tongue—
the goblin's proud, pointed nose
one can't resist touching.

The code of my dream—
No sooner is the mermaid asleep with me
than I suck at her breast;
no sooner am I caught by the river monster
than I swim in the raging water.

Kijima

Raison D'Etre OF RED

One cannot live without stealing fire.

Having played with fire, one knows
inner forms; inner function.
Friends' unknown eyes meet
and the flame twirls up:
or oxygen consumes everything, then disappears.
We become bones of ancient cities on the sea bottom;
we become the musical score for flickering sunbeams.

This time we perform love burning ourselves.

This time . . . this fire in darkness . . . this demon's
    tongue . . . this wick.
Without red, I can never have a color.

Kijima

CATTLE

streaming
a huge belt
herds of cattle
lured out, chased
black, driven to the slaughterhouse
dragged into the freezing granite mouth
trickling, one after another
mucous of finest stickiness
and from the very bottom of this deluge
din, moans, reverberation, doomed melancholy
like the knives of serious children
the black luster of the herds' horns, thrust up, piercing the sky
suddenly, the splash of floating trees leaping up, colliding
even sexual excitement becomes a desperate form of protest
before, behind, jammed in, jumping up, bending over
bulls   steers   cows   calves
unable to gnaw off the invisible halter
deep black, sluggish
irritated backs flowing
to the slaughterhouse as endless
as a huge flooded river
to the slaughter's iron railing
herds of jet black cattle

Kijima

OMEN

fascists don't retreat without destruction

II

Like bodies
chests   skulls
even eyes popped out
crushed by the train
that day
the Japanese archipelago
jostled
like a lava flow,
human groans turned to steam
and serpentine lines of smoke
reached toward the sun.

And an instant later,
no plains
no hills
no cities
everything: a brown-desert-hole, a fossil-skeleton.

(The ruins of private, Imperial bases!)

drifting shadows of dead bodies
remain in the sea
around lead-gray islands

100,000,000,000 . . .   light years

Certainly, space men will send messages of condolence
from the extreme reaches of the galaxy
laughing out loud

. . . PPP(SORRY) . . . RRP(I'M SORRY) . . .
  TPP(VERY SORRY) . . .

III

When can I be guaranteed I'll be able to kick off this dream?

If I should stray over
the ruins of an atomic blast
alone as a ghost,
there would be no way of finding an old acquaintance
except to make a pilgrimage
through layers of the earth's crust
deposited after this devastating abuse of the law of light and matter,
the innermost rule of the forming universe.
If, not knowing how to avoid it,
we were splashed by the genocidal light,
we would engrave our love
on the granite pavement
like a relief of shadows
to show that on this axis of the solar system,
in this country which is nothing
but a cemetery of unknown dead, thousands and thousands
of millions of them, there must have been love.
Dream!—We want our present embrace
to remain as a sign of the breath of people who loved each other
and in memory of immortal innocence,
branded in stone like a Pompeian relic,
but this dream too is empty.

Kijima

FALLING STAR

1949
summer   midday
his leap to death
was like a raindrop leaving no trace on the building's whiteness

but this changed
the flowing pavement
into the glare
of a single focus

Aa!
speeding, cruel primary colors
fall continuously
dissolving all objects in the eyes of gathered people
sepia lines of street lights' lily-shaped lamps
something silvery falling from the sky

there was only one
sane achievement
of stopping his heart
a phrase in his will
written on a crumpled paper in a yellow envelope
    "At least the fate of my class will be my experience alone."

then setting sunlight
showered
and his bone frame
stiffened for an instant
with the weariness of parting
all at once it splashed into abundant ashes
in the crematorium

again and again and again
the dogged memory
of my friend passing through death
like a circus rider
falling upside down

Kijima

ASK AGAIN

What shall I call the present moment?
A year of expectation? Days of spiral stairs?
I was born in the wrong era.
People say, "At the instant   of birth
each of us is sentenced to die.
So we're all pleasantly foolish prisoners of death row."

What shall I call the present moment?
A year of living burial? Days on a howling sea?
I want to see the world after I die.
"Sooner or later you'll see it," someone whispers.
"Oh, yeah? You think you'll see anything after death?"
I want ears without gravity and a parachute's eyes.

What shall I call the present moment?
A year of disbelief? Days in a vortex?
What attracts me whose senses deaden more each day and night?
It's the newness of burning prospects.
My old self may come to life from figures in the ashes.

What shall I call the present moment?
Anyone can reverse and pin splendidly in dreams.
The hangman is hung.

The deifying are deified.
The world is a boomerang,
a boomerang;
boomerang.

Kijima

HONESTY COVERED WITH FLAME

—in memory of John Coltrane—

My and your, and *my* and *your*
evil spells denser than smog:
the moving, silent, unwounded crucified!
Somehow our souls will explode
for those forced to communicate in secret
with the language of the dumb.
How can our freedom be captured
by a wire net of heartbeats in someone's upset eyes?
Burn self-igniting man!
Curious prudence afraid of revolt, GET OUT!

Cruel cities kept hurting you,
tearing you lengthwise and crosswise to heaven
as you roared for man.
    Let riffs from you past
    ring wide and clear!

SHOT DOWN OR SOLD OUT
SOLD OUT OR SHOT DOWN
Shot down or sold out
Sold out or shot down
shot down or sold out

Kijima • 137

sold out or shot down
sold out

Aa!

there
lightning
dashes
everywhere
speed-of-light
touches
TRANE *Trane* trane
wind whirls
glides
stroking wooden walls' grain
birds fly in my palm lines
TRANE *Trane* trane
up from the cruel hours of fossils
to the sky's blue pain   one
                    two
            three
whirling   gliding   wheeling   one
                    two
            three
the flaming spirits of birds
soothing agony's red wounds
whispering to the cool fresh wind
locus of whirling birds; falling, lovely, weird
weird birds swelling into insurrection
ca-caressing thorn   that makes us lively   you too
ci-city planning for slaves   suffering   you too
po-power to dreams   done now   for you

TRAIN crosses
the swamp-dream

cast off,
don't be entwined
by hidden shame
each heart's contour is unique
TRAIN beyond
the swamp-dream

AH, ASCENSION!
Dispersed ashes gulped down
with burning misfortune
are absorbed and digested immediately.
Exactly
at the time of my rebirth I am on top of a mountain.
I am in the ranks of an expedition
guided by your saxophone's erupting visions.

Kijima

THE HAND OF VELOCITY

for Kajiyama Toshio

Can you see an embryo exhausted by singing
in each texture of the ruins?
After feeling destruction beyond the reach of words,
your cyclone-like writing,
which intrudes upon an unexplored self-universe,
opens you pliantly and lets you touch anew,
giving you the freedom to grasp and control everything.
Line drawings of velocity don't show how they were made,
but call me, a sentinel,
but invite me to perform.

Kijima

MESSAGE TO THE FLYING

How far do you think you can fly?
What you were murmuring just now
is the panting approach to a hop, skip and jump.

DO YOU READ ME? OVER

Your fantastic way of jumping
has the speed of your escape from your mother's womb;
is like a caress thrown away in silence.

DO YOU READ ME? OVER

Mechanical lullabies sway you.
Great goal of the young universe,
singing beyond this parabolic line; appear!

DO YOU READ ME? OVER

You are melodies which want to be thrown out;
want to fly out of the gravity where war drools
and life's neurosis repeatedly flows into sleeping infants.

DO YOU READ ME? OVER

To us, half broken receivers;
to us, who devour each other with our eyes;
to us, stuffed animals embracing each other;
to us, hanging in mid-air, unable to make even an emergency
    landing:

DO YOU READ ME? OVER

Kijima

HUMAN AIR

All the winds
    Twirling up
From the heart
    Can be performers

Streams of breath
    Through instruments
Are like blood vessels
    Recently kissed

Fingers that touched
    Glowing tones
Are like lovers who
    Just missed their love

Kijima

SO FREE

Don't get drunk
    On that giddiness pressed
Between ocean and sky
    Train yourself to swim through it

When your muscles burn
    Your mind calms
The breeze on your skin
    Is a deep comfort

Jumping and diving
    All alone

Be attentive to the unmanageable
    Enemy that is you

Kijima

FROM NOW ON

I've seen cruel instigations
The suicide's desolation
The burnt skin   the experimentation at Hiroshima
Death goes back and forth in a moth flying
From now on, what can I see through?

I've seen the fermentation of sin
The responsible act of taking aim
The mind of the pantheist snythesizing dreams
The lie in the drunk speech of the militants
From now on, what can I see through?

I've seen film negatives of the emotions
The unbalanced steps of escaping thieves
The sky elegantly hanging its tongue out
The innumerable whispers pouring into the new bud
From now on, what can I see through?

Kijima

VIE

Without maps in our brain cells,
    Who has not wandered alone?
Can we burrow into any tunnel?

Without gun sights in our brain cells,
Who has not taken aim by himself?
Can we hit any target?

Without a compass in our brain cells,
Who has not navigated alone?
Can we be guided by dreams?

But to fight for the death of selfishness
Though the self is always an axis,
Is to find the way out, at deadlocks.

Kijima

OUTSIDE THE CIRCLE

The words in my song are charged
with permanent magnetism,
penetrating everywhere.
It can't help but attract everyone
who wants to be human.

I want to believe this,
but my words have strict limits
beyond which darkness and light,
good and evil, beauty and truth,
disappear without a trace.

The world my words cannot reach
is infinite, and though that place
holds nothing for me,
clearly magnets are hidden there
and through them my song glitters.

Kijima

ENCOUNTER

for Ruiko and her pictures

In the double, triple circuits of languages that meet
   but never meet
On cold Manhattan Island
Distrust inhabits tall buildings
No place where senses aren't locked in
Diminutive lady, hoping to force open every lock
You walked into the dens where jazz seeped in
You went up to gamboling black kids—
Perfunctory words, flatteries, hidden moanings
Cars, walking solitudes
Overwhelmed that giant labyrinth
Where I met you
We had no keys for each other
I hated the thick doors locked doubly, triply
I was a pilgrim in freezing Manhattan
You led, me, clutching your camera
To churches in Harlem, to midnight jazz bars
You took photos, each photo a soft breath
Your lens groped through the labyrinth, the dark
In search of people who wanted to be people
I felt your desire to give a gentle hug to each one
In the labyrinth overwhelmed with solitude
Your every shot was a smile
A greeting, a light, to the people, stirring
To reassure themselves, unseen—
On freezing Manhattan Island
We met, without keys

Sato

144 •

HASEGAWA RYUSEI 1928–

Born in Osaka. After various employment, he now works for an advertising company, and writes stories and film criticism. He was a member of the poetry group, "Retto" (Archipelago). *Tiger* was published in 1960.

THE PURSUER

Now in your living room in America,
Or on that island in the Pacific,
No matter. I'll find you.
What's your name?
When did you take off, that day, from the island?
And the names of your co-pilots?
August 6 at 9:30 a.m.
From the high sky of Hiroshima,
You let loose the first atom bomb
Killing with light hundreds of thousands
Of civilians, burning them with so much light.
Over the mushroom cloud you flew back at ease.
You had a celebratory drink.
And the booze. Was it clear or cloudy?
After all, this is war. You don't mind forgetting it all.
Or were you giddy with success?
I'll find out. I'm eager to learn.
Who were all of you?
How could you take this soul-shaking action?
You say, "An order's an order."
Who was it, what character ordered,

How was this "order" transmitted?
Your C.O. would say
You'd better obey it. It's absolute.
Show me some Absolutes:
The pilots, the senior officers.
Whose hands held such power over your own?
Tell me the guy's name.
Let's go to see these men in power,
These in the Strategic Air Command.
Think deeply. Name them.
And who ran the super agency that put on the show?
Let's name it.
Generals, cabinet ministers, technicians.
The names of all the capitalists, the names of the war scientists
Who stood behind their product: the holocaust.

None of you
Feels any guilt.
In every state in America
There are thousands of churches.
And on the bald scar of the blast they built a church.
But your violence is stronger.
You order, one after another,
The second, the third, the fourth atom bomb.
The commander transmits the command down the line
To the last select sadists who board the plane
And kill thousands of humans
For profit, only for your profit.
A good blast widens your market.

But you contradict yourself.
You cannot exterminate the human race.
You cannot erase all of us.

Who are we?
We're the pursuers, the hunters.
We are judges who examine your lives.
We add up the crimes and the spilled blood.

Survivors of Hiroshima,
It is pointless to grieve, exhibiting
Your wounds to no one.
Let's find the criminals.
Let's get down to the core.
Who were they all?
However we're killed, tortured,
This history of hunting does not stop.
The number of pursuers grows as history
Continues. The pursuers grow
Sharper, they stand out, they
Preside over the Last Judgment.

I am the pursuer,
We are the hunters then,
We blow out the fires of curses.

Kijima

PAVLOV'S CRANES

Beating sturdy feathers,
exerting the power of flight,
severing and rebounding
the mist in space,
their oars, wings, a single motion,
thousands of migrant birds, their vibrations

Hasegawa • 147

begin to echo in the depth of my ear.
Common cranes perhaps, sarus cranes or storks,
hard to distinguish,
Pavlov's odd wing-beats,
in the sky of the quiet cerebrum, of the night,
like the water split aside by pectoral fins
of gleaming fish in flight,
through my skin, continually,
echo, come closer.

From the marshes of despair
they've flown up;
and hazarding the night
or heading toward daybreak,
Pavlov's strange cranes,
a hundred or so in each group,
have started their energetic move.
Each, its green beak tilted upward,
its weight resting
on the tail of the crane before it,
balancing power,
gliding through currents of air,
forming a line,
they fly.

The one heading the group,
it's a lump of resistance and exhaustion.
But successively
they replace the leader,
the leader, successively
in neat order, falls back to the end of the flock;
constructing a balance,
drawing a small half-circle,

a line of space,
they fly splendidly.

Have you seen it:
it is always touched and led
at the surface of the reflex-bow.
Night's cerebrum. It's on the sea of the occipital
    cerebral cortex.
Hazarding nihilism
or heading toward daybreak,
thousands of Pavlov's cranes,
a hundred or so in each group,
migrate as if challenging.
All the hundred birds, beaks tilted upward,
weight resting on tails before them,
in a line, silent,
never cease.

Sato

SUMMER MUSHROOM

Midsummer. In the forest
on a dry pass small as a cave
tens of thousands of ants
are lined up one after another
here they come
the mouths of the ants that go one way
are empty, but
the mouths of the ants that return
clutch green leaves
they chew the leaves as they carry them

they scatter them in a 300 cubic meter underground nursery
handed down from generation to generation
in the dark castle of the ant hill
a long time has gone by now
crushed and scattered leaves
have begun rotting
a mesh of small white cabbage-headed mushrooms
covers it lightly as mist
they are the summer mushrooms
no one has seen

Ayusawa

MY BURIAL SONG

Corpses of worker ants
with six extremities
fastened to each body
never wake from their sleep
worker ants carry the corpses
in two columns
I saw them bury each corpse
in an individual grave
I put a few corpses
in a test tube
in an artificial nest
in a moment the ants had carried these corpses
to their graves
the terrible ant called formica sanguinaria
has slaves and lets them carry their corpses
to a place far from
the miserable grave of slaves

my corpse left Munda Islandia
under cover of night
on the deck of Takasago-maru
piled high with the remains of beaten troops
from boats rolling over in waves
using a long hook
the ambulance corps set aside
dead bodies
from bodies choking blood, pus, infected
by maggots
when the ship got under way
someone poured out oil
and set the corpses on fire
corpses were tossed into
three blast furnaces
on the red cross ship
one after another
onto the dazzling bones
perfect combustion wore veils like insect wings
when the fire flared
the heavy door closed
My corpse however didn't flame up
but began to decay and reek

I scratched a tiny wound on my chest
which began to fester
and pulled out maggots and viscera
smeared with a scab's pus,
the place for burial is already prepared
and I must drag my remains
before the prime minister
and the chief of police

of the terrible species formica sanguinaria
so my remains begin walking
from the hair of viscera carried on my shoulder
a yellow serum drips and trails behind me

Ayusawa

HAND OF DEATH

So there's a boy.
But his dream is rejected.
On the great overhead railway
a large bridge is a rainbow.
Broken in two places
its ends emerge touching skyscrapers.
Skyscrapers of many cyclinders.
Smooth rings of light flow out of them.
The helicopters which take off at night,
canals linked together,
steamships which glide over the land,
a plan for an underground factory—
all these are beaten flat
quite easily.
The boy closes the thin Japanese science magazine of 1998.
What place is this?
The mirror reversing in the boy's small brain
throws light on reality at a 180 degree angle.
Everything is too damp;
even pus seeps from the dried skin of his father's corpse.
The limping boy folds his father's body in thirds,

puts it in a box,
takes it down the dark stairs,
ties it on the back of his rattling bicycle
and carries it off at night
to the place of burning.

Ayusawa

FUKUI HISAKO 1929–

Born and lives in Kobe City. A
graduate of Kansai Gakuin University,
she teaches at Kobe Yamate Womens
Junior College, and has published five
volumes of poetry. *Fruit and Knife* was
published in 1958.

IF THE TIME TO DIE COMES TO ME

'Mama
If the time to die comes to me
I hope you'll tell me in a loud voice
Death is like the sea,
The whale's way;
On a hill where dead plankton
Is falling like snow,
A huge tomb lies.
Tell me it's the place
Where any man from any country
Bathing in the spray splashed by whales
May have a fresh dream.

'It does not resemble the dreams
Of those curious South Sea shells
Or the tropical fish with its luminous spinal stripes.
But it suggests the thing
Which we never might have seen in our lives,
Nor can remember,
Although we have glimpsed it.

'Yes, Mama,
It's not a tree, a fish, a butterfly, or a crawfish.
But it's the thing
Like the breaking sea spray.
It's the thing,
Itself a profoundly heavy spray.
Therefore
Let me sink into the sea
And hear the whales' laughter.'

Fukui

FRUIT AND KNIFE

You walk around holding a knife.
At a fruit stand
Or in an orchard
In a book if you like,
You can find fruit.

When you flourish your intense will to kill
A bare fruit will roll out.
The way of cutting it is so bracing
That the neat parings
May force you to feel agreeable
But

If there should be a moment
When your hot sweat on the knife handle
Fails to show your usual skill,
There will roll out Cézanne's fruit,
Which will have something to do with you.

Fukui • 155

It's impossible with a knife.
For the fruit is crooked;
Crookedness itself is a fruit.

Fukui

A BOAT

You, a boat
You don't float on the water,
Much less are embraced by water.
You are struggling with water.
Each moment
You continue strained to the dazzling point
Against water seeping in.
With its terrible power
The water pulls you on,
And you cling to its surface.
The strong wind,
Swinging and
Swelling the sails
Invites you to the sky
—Are white clouds flying in the air ghosts or friends?
Yet you run
You exist on the water's surface.
Between the sky and sea
When the garboard and the water touch,
You live.

Fukui

YOUR WORDS

Pick up and gather
Your words
And put them
In a sack.
If I threw them out carelessly,
They would become knives
And join in stabbing me.
They would reveal the hidden wounds
And renew their pains.
Finally
Having left me bloodstained
They would make me unable to see you,
So that the words would be pleased.
Yet what I want to see is you
Not around you.
As soon as the words are spoken, then
Quickly I will hide myself
Opening the sack's mouth.

Fukui

TWO TABLEAUS

1

It seems running through the dark woods at full speed
Is living a madness;
A disgusting smell rising from the damp marsh,
Out of the rocks drops of water counting time,
Gnarled laughter which the roots vent,

Audible and horrible voices from somewhere—
They say that a branch is bleeding.
What would it feel like to dry up blood
And to be bark
Like a girl who escaped from Apollo?
Would it seem to be the swallowing of a green plum
Or the feeling of ecstasy and nirvana as a water lotus blooms?

2

In the woods
The night does not move.
Only the pebbles touched by the faint light and the foot are
    decisive.
The animals hiding in the brush
The moths fluttering their powdered wings
Will appear to the walker as conspirators in the same insanity.
The leaves peep with their open eyes
And take good seats like a stenographer in a council house.
In the woods where the air stirs
Like a theatre just before the raising of the curtain
From somewhere one can hear
The tune of a flute.

Fukui

OOKA MAKOTO 1931–

Born in Mishima City, Middle Japan. He graduated from Tokyo University, with a major in Japanese literature. He was a reporter for ten years for the Yomiuri Press. He translated Paul Eluard, and writes radio and TV scripts and art criticism. His published essays include *Art and Tradition*. He teaches Japanese literature at Meiji University. He was a member of the poetry group, "Kai" (Oars). *Memory and Presence* was published in 1956.

CORAL ISLAND

1

On the horizon made by our approaching lips
In the burning words on our hollow palms
Under the crater between our bodies
We secretly bury
Soul's Siamese twins
Where life and death embrace each other

Under the serene October air
Life's stream changes into smooth skin
of a lake of death
And each man becomes
a Night
carrying a mirror in its heart

O Sun
Our sprouting bulb
stuck on our sky's surface.

    2

Bird!
Heart's volcanic bomb.
Pupil of autumn piercing the wind's roofs.

Tree!
Burning hair in the bottom of the earth.
Melting fingertips of lovers.

City!
Remnants-filled dining table of gods.
Disappearing silence.

Then man sinks
through the deep tunnel of sleep's stream
Torn off from himself like flower petals

But I always remain an island
If the sun penetrates into my forest of shells
I become a transparent coral island
A foaming crest of love.

Ooka

"A MAN WITHOUT A GRAIN OF SENTIMENT"

A man without a grain of sentiment
    crosses the winter River Sumida
        towards a universe without love
            without birds.

A man without a grain of courage
   his lungs filled with tar
      washes a child's neck by the River Sumida
         flooded by hopeless evening sun.

I have made a long journey
   a distance thirty years cannot measure
      with no one but women
         fallen on their sides.

I am trying to come near
   a protean invisible city
      made probably of winds
         a city of pains where men begin to bear children.

I do not believe in the conqueror's goodwill
   cannot believe in the malice
      of the betrayed class.
         Please at last

leave untouched
innocence about to be born.

Sato

TO LIVE

Do they know
that water has many levels:
the fish at the bottom
and the hornwort drifting on the surface
receive different lights
which make them multi-colored
give them many shadows

I find pearls on the pavements
I live   in the woods of images
on the musical notes spanning my heart's threads
I live   in the holes drops make on the snow
in the morning swamp where liverwort blooms
I live   on a map of past and future

I've forgotten the color my eyes were yesterday
but what my eyes saw yesterday
my fingers know
and because what the eyes saw has been touched
like beech skin touched by hands
I live   on the sense, the flesh, being
    blown in the wind

Sato

FAMILY

Mother is a river,
father is a lone tree
on an island:
fields do not belong to him.
Midnight when the garden collapses
and returns to the domain of mud,
the child, shooting
sharp stone arrowheads,
goes back to night's deep woods,
to a mist-closed, viviparous grave
where the blood of ferocious birth
slowly turns solid,
where the child remains

a blind light,
a buzzing silence,
a wheel at a standstill turning violently.
The wave-tossing death-sea
is far down the mother, the river.

The memory of flood
is the memory of birth.
The child had begun, already in the pain of swimming,
to imitate the ichthyoid.
He will grow through imitation,
expand the illusion to develop his perspective.
But when his love can't feel the knife biting into the flesh
and his eyes are chewed apart by sand of order
    shifting constantly,
he will thirst, scream,
demand war.

When that happens, will his father,
like past fathers,
have to keep for him, in the garden,
a water buffalo,
which is too gentle for the world?

Sato

TANIKAWA SHUNTARO 1931–

Born in Tokyo. He graduated from Tokyo Municipal Toyotama High School, and writes radio scripts, plays, and short short stories. He published the essays, *To The World*, and participated in making the documentary film of the Tokyo Olympiad. His lyrics have been set to music by many musicians. He was a member of the poetry group, "Kai" (Oars). *Twenty Billion Light Years of Loneliness* was published in 1952.

GROWTH

Drawing a meaningless line,
a child says it's an apple.

Painting an apple just like an apple,
a painter says it's an apple.

Painting an apple unlike an apple,
an artist says it's truly an apple.

Not painting an apple or anything else
members of the Academy of Art
slurp up apple sauce.

Apples, apples, red apples,
are apples bitter? Are they sour?

Wright

MUSEUM

stone axes and the like
lie quietly behind the glass

constellations rotate endlessly
many of us become extinct
many of us appear

then
comets endlessly miss collision
lots of dishes and the like are broken
Eskimo dogs walk over the South Pole
great tombs are built both east and west
books of poems are often dedicated
recently
the atom's being smashed to bits
the daughter of a president is singing
such things as these
have been happening

stone axes and the like
lie absurdly quiet behind the glass

Wright

PICNIC TO THE EARTH

here let's jump rope together   here
here let's eat balls of rice together
here let me love you
your eyes reflect the blueness of sky
your back will be stained a wormwood green
here let's learn the constellations together

from here let's dream of every distant thing
here let's gather low-tide shells,
from the sea of sky at dawn
let's bring back little starfish
at breakfast we will toss them out
let the night be drawn away

here I'll keep saying, "I am back."
while you repeat, "Welcome home."
here let's come again and again
here let's drink hot tea
here let's sit together for awhile
let's be blown by the cooling breeze.

Wright

CYCLE OF MONTHS
(MENSTRUATION)

1

within her someone prepares a banquet
within her someone carves an unknown son
within her someone is wounded

2

the palm of god,
injured clumsily in the act of creation,
still finds it difficult to forget

3

"with such accurate regularity   florid
funerals occur within me   they are

mourned in the color of celebration   they
continue, unwounded and unable to die, to
return to nothingness   my children who
are overly young . . . a ripe moon is
falling   there is no one to receive it
I am waiting   I am alone squatting
in a chilly place and waiting—
for someone to sow the moon
for someone to deprive me of this rising tide—
with a wound, lost to the memory
of all, within me that is outside the
reach of healing"

   4

. . . while alluring those who will to live
towards the shore   the tide flows full
within her   there within her lies a sea
calling to the moon   and as the moon
revolves around   there lies within her an
endless calendar . . .

Wright

HANDS

hands
they feel
hips of women
hands
they tease
hair of boys

hands
they squeeze
hammers
hands of friends
hands they seize
daggers
hemlines of lives

hands
they strike
a father's face
hands
they stroke
inkslabs
hands
they create
they destroy
they take
hands
they give
they hold
hands
they release
they open
hands
they close
hands

ceaselessly do something
ceaselessly do nothing

hands
they indicate in vain
thickly luxuriantly
like leaves in summer

hands
wide open they wither

Wright

BILLY THE KID

First a little dirt on my mouth and slowly big clods of earth
between my legs and over my gut   an ant whose nest was
smashed crawls quietly over my closed eyelids   the folks
have stopped crying and seem to be feeling good in the sweat
of their shoveling   in my chest there's two holes drilled by a
soft-eyed sheriff   my blood spurted from the two paths of
escape   then I really realized that blood wasn't mine   I knew
that my blood, me and my blood, were headed on
back   above me the only enemy I ever had   the dry blue
sky   it's taken everything from me   even on the run   even
as I shot   even while loving it, the blue sky that kept taking
from me, in the end, failed to take from me only one
time   the time of my death   now I have nothing to be taken
from me   now at last I don't fear the blue sky   I don't fear
that silence or that endless blue   since now I'm being taken
away by the ground   I can go back to where I can't be reached
by the hands of the blue sky, to where I can live without
fighting   now my cries will be answered   now the sounds of
my gun will linger in my ears   now when I can no longer
hear or can no longer shoot!

Tanikawa • 169

In killing, I tried to make sure of men and myself   my
youthful way of proving was studded in colors of blood   but
with the blood of other men I couldn't paint away the blue
sky   I needed my own blood   I got it today   I made sure
my own blood clouded over the blue sky and then returned to
the ground   so now I can no longer see the blue sky or even
remember it   I smell the smell of my ground, now I am
waiting to become the ground   above me the wind is
blowing   I no longer envy the wind   soon I will become the
wind   then soon without even knowing the blue sky I will
live in the blue sky   I'll become a lone star   and know all the
nights   and know all the days   still turning around and
around as a star.

Wright

BEGGAR

I was asked why I was silent,
it was just because there was no way to say it
     except by being silent.
They beat me,
broke my crutches,
and killed my little brown dog.
I laughed. So I am an eternal beggar,
and right before all the good citizens
I'll remain crouched
     and live on forever.

Wright

DOG

Sadder than myself
there is a dog
there—
down the alley
silent
cowering
only his eyes are wide open
nobody calls him
nobody notices him
when I am sad
sadder than myself,
there is a dog
always
there
beside me
never begging for pity,
merely
there.

Wright

ADHERENCE TO APPLES

It can't be called red, it's not color but apple.
It can't be called round, it's not shape but apple.
It can't be called sour, it's not taste but apple.
It can't be called expensive, it's not price but
apple. It can't be called pretty, it's not beauty
but apple. It can't be classified, it's not a plant,
but because it's an apple.

Tanikawa • 171

Blooming apples. Ripening apples. Apples on branches
swaying in the wind. Rained upon apples, pecked
upon apples, picked off apples. Apples fallen upon
the ground. Rotten apples. Apple seeds, sprouting
apples. Apples useless to refer to as apples. Apples
that aren't apples, apples that are apples, apples that
are or aren't, simple one apple is all apples.

McIntosh, Delicious, Baldwin, Jonathan, Winesap, Northern Spy,
a single apple, three or five or a dozen
or seven kilos of apples, twelve tons
of apples or two million tons of apples. Production
of apples, transported apples. Measured, packaged,
bought and sold apples. Sterilized apples, digested
apples, consumed apples, vanished apples.
Apples! Apples?

That, that over there, that there. There
that there, that in a basket. That falling
from the table, that copied on canvas,
that baked in an oven. Children take it in their
hands and nibble it, that, it. Despite
the number eaten, despite the number rotten, they
spring one after another from branches, that which
gleamingly, endlessly, overflow shops. A replica of what?
A replica of when?

Unable to answer, they are apples. Unable to ask,
they are apples. Unable to tell, after all they are
apples, still . . .

Wright

ADULT TIME

A child in a week
becomes a week smarter.
A child in a week
learns fifty new words.
A child in a week
can bring change to himself.
An adult in a week
is the same as before.
An adult in a week
turns over the same weekly.
An adult takes a week
merely to scold a child.

Wright

FANTASY STATISTICS

BROKEN BRANCHES: Eight million six hundred twenty-one thousand
and three.

INJURED BUTTERFLIES: Five hundred thirteen thousand four hundred
and twenty-one.

BORN GENIUSES: Minus three.

UNTIED RIBBONS: Sixty-nine thousand five hundred and fifteen meters.

FLOWN TEARS: Five hundred and eight million cubic meters.

INNOCENT MEN: Zero.

SNEEZES: Incalculable.

Tanikawa • 173

FADED RAINBOWS: Just the number of men who have gotten married.

BROKEN KETTLEDRUMS: Four.

PLATONIC LOVE: 8½

REGRETTABLE SITUATIONS: Infinitely large.

ME: Just one.

Wright

HOMEWORK

When I closed my eyes
I could see god.

If I opened my squinted eyes
god became invisible.

I open my eyes wide
and whether I can see god or not,
that's my homework.

Kijima

SONNET 41

I open my eyes into blue sky
and feel there's a place for my return,
but the light that comes through clouds
can't make it back up.

What the generous sun casts out
we gather in busily, even after dark.
People are born greedy,
never resting like the rich trees.

My window cuts away what overflows.
The room I want is the universe,
so I don't get along with other people.

My living injures space and time,
and their pain falls back on me.
Only if I leave will I feel well again.

Bean

ODDLY ENOUGH

When we go to the sea: mountainous waves, jellyfish and cholera
    germs are waiting.
When we go to the mountains: landslides, a fall, and man-eating
    bears.
When we go along the road: hit-and-run drivers, collisions, thieves.
When we stay home: burglars, taxmen and double suicides.
And everywhere else: earthquakes, hurricanes and volcanic erup-
    tions.
If not: revolutions, civil war and plane crashes.
Experiments in nuclear fission.
as well as psychiatric patients
are left to take care of themselves.
Nevertheless . . .
How strange, how miraculous,

I am alive and flourishing!
Under the sun at 95°,
a good balance between sweat and beer.

Atsumi

MAMA

Earth, clutching at a jet plane,
Tries to hug it to her breast.

Earth, absorbing a submarine,
Tries to return it to her sea's womb.

Fat-headed mama
Is jealous of the universe.

Earth, never changed,
Drags at our departing feet

Though we'll soon be in puberty;
The age to touch the moon.

Atsumi

MARIJUANA

Sweat smarts my eyes.
Blood boils in my fingertips.
Slobber at my lips.
In a sax's sex a bubbling slobber's success.
In the middle of irritated rhythms looking for a heart
I search for an image:

an old broken banjo
a spear slashing the sky
the sundial at Venice
the Virgin walking
a door with crumbled varnish
Christopher Columbus
the sea swaying
history that keeps shedding blood
fifteen cups of coffee.
I look for my face there.
I look for love.

Gigantic roots spread
to unknown ends.
At the ends of branches that grow and wither on the earth
innumerable corpses hang.
They soon fall to the ground. Underneath
the gigantic roots spread.

Lento

COOL

It is cold here.
It is cold here, Miles.
Though I have my wife and kids, Miles,
it is cold.
You are a cool Negro, Miles.
Don't leave me alone.
Don't desert our civilization.
It is cold, Miles, and
you are cool.

Your murmur through your thick lips is cool,
cooler than any abstract art in a New York gallery.
It is cooler than a stuckup French fashion model's kiss.
Ah, modern living.
It is cold here.
Though I have stocks, my car and my villa
it is cold here.
You are a cool Negro, Miles.
You disgrace us with your pink blood.
You pat us softly with the fair inside of your hand.
I have Bach and Rembrandt, but
you were born out of Bongo's womb,
brought up at the blue creek's bottom:
you tell your own fortune with cards in a whorehouse in Harlem:
and you look at me.
It is cold here.
No more with your gentle mute.
Play me in place of your pet, Miles.
Warm me, soak me with your breath.
I will leave my girl blond all over in the elevator.
Mark my penthouse in your black new map.

You are a cool Negro, Miles
I will lynch you.
It is not cold here.
I have everything.

Lento

YASUMIZU TOSHIKAZU 1931–

Born and lives in Kobe City. He graduated from Kobe University with a major in English contemporary poetry. He is a member of the literary group, "Taurus," and writes radio scripts continuously. He has published eight volumes of poetry. *Songs for Being* was published in 1955.

THE FLOWERS OF THE ROCK

In a village where the west wind rages,
overlapping waves roll in;
roofs are always wet,
and it is wet under the roofs,
and cold.

Firewood was piled and burned on the beach
although a man's body lies there only half burned.
The boat he came in smashed on a jutting rock in the offing
and not a halyard remains.

March
Camellia flowers like blood
April
Snowstorms blown sideways like bad memories
May
At last the dazzling sea
August
Black flowers on the rock

Afternoon like a battlefield:
a barefoot girl
skipped around on the rock
and picked the rock's flowers for me.
When I told her I wanted to plant them in my garden,
the girl looked at me with round, black eyes.
    "The thing I hate most
    is a quarrel among friends
    caused by strangers.
    Hatred rots in the heart,
    rots endlessly. These flowers can only bloom
    in this rock's crevice."
She looked at me as if I were the enemy.

The black flowers in my hand have no where to go.
The girl's red, chapped mouth has no where to go in my memory.

Kobayashi

FABLE OF THE BIRD

Many things happen,
and somehow, one by one,
we overcome them.
At the end,
we feel all the worse for it.
Why?
When it's done,
one sighs with relief:
there's a blank page,
a colophon,

another blank page
(or an ad);
bang it shut and another book is finished.
When we make a box,
or take part in sex, it's the same thing.
To feel something is finished hurts:
it means to erase everything that happened,
a let-down to emptiness.
And therefore, the story of the bird
that warmed the snake's egg is a nice story.
The brood egg was a snake's egg,
and the bird brooded over it with all her heart,
giving her warmth to it,
gulping in the time.
When the egg hatched,
the snake opened its mouth wide
and swallowed the bird;
a superfluous conclusion.
A conclusion preceded by blind selfishness.
A conclusion followed by foolish indifference.
Perhaps, in this way,
we can secretly learn
of slightly abnormal feelings.
One hot, summer day
at Taos, Lawrence,
impatient with a hen that wanted to brood,
cut off her head with a hatchet.
The headless chicken, it is said,
walked back to her eggs.

Kobayashi

SAY YOU ARE LOVELY

What reason not to
call you lovely?
But words are insanely perverse and jealous,
displeased with our relationship.
They don't want to
flow between us.
So listen a moment.
Why not trick
words?
Let me throw the word *lovely*
into your lovely mouth,
and seal it inside your lovely lips
tightly, with my lips.
The word will die in furious agony
in your mouth,
and after it dies,
if love survives;
would you mind?

Kijima

SONG

When I look into your eyes
my world is a thorn bush.
Frantically, like children,
birds try to escape.
Their feathers decorate branches.
The earth accepts these naked birds.

When I look into your eyes
my world is a lake whose waters can't escape.
Frantically, fish scatter
like children.
Their glittering scales sink.
The lake bottom accepts the naked fish.

If suddenly, before your eyes,
I opened my world,
would you faint
with a child's cry of wonder?
Or, just then, would you accept me,
naked.

Kijima

SHIRAISHI KAZUKO 1931–

Born in Vancouver, Canada. She was
educated in Japan, where she moved at the
age of seven, and was graduated from the
Faculty of Literature of Waseda Univer-
sity. She published the essays, *Loves, Gods,
and Animals*, and writes fiction and criti-
cism. *Tiger's Play* was published in 1960.

MY TOKYO

I, like Buddha,
Almost sitting on this city
Am now pregnant with the ennui of October.

My dearest girl friend, naked,
Walks up and down in an attic in New York;
Hysterically vivacious.

Wrapping an arm around Masuo's neck
You'll ask for kisses.
I want to touch, stripping it from its picture-frame,
That thin, coquettish, white nude body.
It will be very white, white as chalk,
A desolate sea yet solid.
It must, at touching, flake,
Letting small rolls of dirty plaster fall.
I see the thick pants of an Italian
Who, on his shoulders, totes you to the scullery in a washing-bag.
The empty cans of cheap beer which he bought
Lie in the first-floor bar.
They squeak like rats.
It is America. America the Hungry.

My dumb October,
Such sullenness of concrete
Hangs around My Tokyo.
Faked tears of false mankind, annoyingly,
Rustle about to no purpose. Lipsalves
Flood from the juke-box and then turn
To shoals of small sardines, give out bad smells
And find their way to be artistic and poetic thought.

O usual academic autumn!
Saying byebye to all of them,
I, after a long time,
Enter my inward canal:
I smuggle myself into my inner city.
At the entrance to that city, at the end of summer,
I met an individual,
Amen-hotep, Pharoah of ancient Egypt.
He was an unknown youth, nowadays a bus conductor,
A butcher, a driver of racing cars, a poet, a revolutionary, others
    such,
All the rain (which is not all), the antiquity of Egypt
Of five thousand years ago, a king, an eagle amulet,
Guts of the newborn crocodile for bait, soft brains
Of an infant, perfumed oil for the rituals, pliant dress
Of hatred, Time, which is a part of them and all of them.

I, hand in hand with a moment of Amen-hotep,
In and out of such chaos
Dashed into a season of personal performance.
At that time
There came the noise of a subway train
Rushing through the bottom of my city womb,
And, on the stage, drums and the bass were sounding.

Sandra began to dance.
Sandra Dressed-all-in-black is not Salome
But a beautiful Lesbian negress, middle class,
A sweet most dissolute mistress, a go-go dancer,
A black St. Mary who turned her husband
Into a pale shark, a eunuched Don Juan.

That I started taking the subway
Led to my first meeting with Henry Miller.
In the chamber pot, in newspapers, old letters, chairs, in milk,
In all the furniture or food
I saw his water waiting to be drunk, cell-bodies
And his rag-like life.

I remain a constant subway-rider.
For hours, almost as long as intercourse,
I have loved the subway. My subway is
No longer made of iron. It's a shape of softest flesh,
A phantom of civilization, a cradle of thought
In that inward city. That subway is
The innermost gut of meditation.
Men who settled in the city
Clung to its ulcer between sleep and waking,
Men incessantly frothing at the mouth;
Not words, not angry roars, not pleadings and not smiles,
Not even courtship, not contentment, not contentiousness:
Nothing but foam.

At the club "so what" at one o'clock in the morning
Max Roach beating a drum.
Why is he so handsome?
Why does his drum appeal so lyrically?
A rain of strong crushing sounds

Are the crown of his technique!
The people there were numbed. They were enchanted.
A microcosm of his music knocked down flat
The idle egg-laying of the people.

My Tokyo,
This city is almost
Our womb.
I, standing at the entrance,
Kissed my Amen-hotep.
Then rain began to fall and we,
For almost all the time of our solidarity, died or united. . . .
To be dead for five thousand years and to be born for five thousand
    years,
To yawn for five thousand years and to keep laughing for five
    thousand years:
It will be more than love.
Everything, frogs, eggs, jam, a piece of blue sky,
Carbon paper, records as well as flies. . . .
Let's dive to the sheets!:
It is the password of our city.
With a dead cat someone in deep solitude so dived.
Someone, too, handsome as he was,
Broke the mirror into pieces, clasped
With all his strength his penis over it and fainted.
Somebody again, being constantly afraid of his delicate
Brain and body, taking the powder of the summer plum,
Crouched on the bed-sheets crying bitterly.
These men, like two young leopards,
Embrace each other quietly in the deep woods of their yearning.
Those beautiful monkey-women in each other's secret rooms
Balance a rainbow of caresses like the glow of morning.

About that time
My personal performance lasted
Quickly and displeasingly, from October to December.
At that time I was caught in the spider-web
Of mere forgetfulness, acute delights, meditative madnesses and so
    forth.
Much of my self fell victim to that spider:
Captured with slovenly cries
One of my selves escaped,
Took the subway and still
Tried to make some sort of music.

This may not be love,
Merely the greetings of the season;
However,
Something was at least committed to music
And I myself, already daubed in the new melody,
Hear my tail lash with the fury of the crocodile of hatred.
But who is being slapped?
Who is this ghost that is summoned into music?

O!
I see Joe in the guise of a ghost at the terminal.
He, already crushed beneath the sexual roller,
Has turned into a grey shadow.
Is he magnetic sand driven into the spermless desert,
Forsaken even by the last drop of his life's storage?
He, caught in the coils of a viper,
Is gradually carried by the spider
Away from the limb of his will.
Already rusted fast into the side of delayed time,
He's going to lower the last curtain.

And I am also
Poking the hot will in the ashes
That I may bury My City completely.
Vaguely I heard God's pain.
After struggling through the fog of premonition
It suddenly changed into a shooting pain.
Now for the first time
I see entire God fall into a thunderbolt, roaring,
To become hot at my side.
It is both momentary and aeon's long:
To lie half-suffering half-injured
In the guise of a feeble traveler.

My city is now
Far off in the distance.
Turning close to the stranger's visage,
It sleeps an aimless sleep
With its neck of concrete drooped.

Atsumi

PHALLUS

                    —for Sumiko's birthday

God exists, though he doesn't exist
And, humorous as he is,
He resembles a certain kind of man.

This time,
Bringing a gigantic phallus,
He joined the picnic
Above the horizon of my dream.

By the way
I regret
I didn't give Sumiko something for her birthday:
But at least I would now wish
To implant the seeds of that God-brought phallus
In the thin, small, charming voice of Sumiko
At the other end of the telephone.

Forgive me, Sumiko,
But the phallus shooting up day by day
Now grows in the heart of the cosmos
And, like a damaged bus, cannot be moved.
Therefore
If you want to see
The beautiful sky with its bright star-spangle
Or some man other than this God-brought phallus,
A man who dashes out in a car
Along the highway with a hot girl,
Then you must really
Hang out of the bus window
And peep about.

When the phallus
Begins to move and comes to the side of the cosmos
It commands a most splendid view. In such a time,
Dear Sumiko,
The loneliness of the way in which the starred night shines
And the curious coldness of midnoon
Thrill me to the marrow.
What is seen is seen whole-heartedly. No man
But goes mad.
Because a phallus has neither name nore personality
And is timeless,

It sometimes leaves its traces
On the tumbled air
When someone passes by
Carrying it uproariously like a portable shrine.
In that hum of voices
One hears the expansion of savage
Disturbance, the imprecations
Of semen not yet ruled by God. Sometimes
God is apt to be absent:
He seems to go somewhere else
Leaving debts or a phallus behind him.

Now
The phallus abandoned by God
Comes this way.
Being young and gay
And full of clumsy confidence
It, surprisingly, resembles the shadow
Of an experienced smile.

The phallus seems to grow beyond all numeration,
And, beyond counting, comes this way.
It is in fact in the singular. It comes alone.
Seen from whatever horizon,
It has nor face nor words.
I would like to give you, Sumiko,
Such a thing for your birthday.

When therewith your whole life is enswaddled,
You will become invisible to yourself.
Occasionally you will turn into the will of the very phallus
And wander endlessly.

I would wish to catch in my arms,
Endlessly,
One such as you.

Atsumi

THE LION'S HUMMING

I was a lion yesterday
humming in the jungle   At night
the stars fell simultaneously
and trampling moonlight
I was burned everywhere
the tip of my nose abraded
my life scorched dangerously by love
and my mane blew somewhere in the wind
to the past   to the future   to death
It flew to eternity
Now my ears and tail
will not come back to me again

Today   coming home from school
I passed a mirror shop
and I could only remember this:
since I forgot my tweezers in the jungle
I can't pick out
a single phrase I was humming

Bean

NON-STOP

The man who started running
cannot stop
Neck thrust out from a building window
Just so! He gallops down the wall
runs down the highway   and when the sea cuts the highway
he runs on the sea
I alone tend the man who can't sleep
who continues running
over notebooks   through drawers
inside my darkness

The man who continues running
forgets to let me sleep
so my days are exhausted
and my nights   stretched out   will not return

Bean

MY AMERICA

I had a phone call
My darling, I want to see you
America is a darling
There's no need to think
Damn hypocrite Jonathan!
I have no interest in politicians
It's a darling I'm interested in
Dearest America
My love

What's your name?
O America
No, you are nothing but you
Your sweat shining in anonymity
Shining love
The barbecue you cook
At the bottom of a love-overflowing bottle
That irresistibly tasty mire
It was far better in bed
I like the inside of your thigh
Gods are overwhelmed
By your reticent, tough and elegant penis
Prayers should be chanted
At a time like this

A kiss good night
After watching the late-night show on TV
Before creeping into bed
I take out a kiss or a canned beer from the freezer
It is always at such a time that I'm puzzled
Which to come first
In the morning
You get up
Your breakfast has a taste
Of the sun, canned goods
Restriction and frozen freedom
You are generous with those flavors

You get angry
Only when you lose money on the races
Everytime you do the shopping
At the supermarket
They give you a pool-ticket

And you pool them   On Saturday night
All in front of TV
Wanting to be an American millionaire
Showing your teeth
Wear the face of
Individualism, egoism
Money-adorationism and optimism
The washing is often snatched
I can't hang it out to dry outside
Though it is not
A slum here
Shut up!
The "Noseopen" is now galloping
The third, the third   ah . . .

I took a trip
To North Dakota   a small country
Smaller than Harajuku
A henhouse-like airport
The smell of oil from the propeller plane
Soaked through the flight lunch sandwiches
We went down the ladder   and then
All at once
People looked at me
Me
And my man

Dark soft hat, dark sunglasses
Dark coat, dark face, and dark hands
But it's not a shadow
Living warm blood-smelt   my
Dark man
Has been waiting for a long time

Shiraishi • 195

For about eternity
Becoming a black point
Here among white faces

Snowflakes are dancing in the sky
Drier than sand. . . .
Noko keeps laughing till she cries
Gil embraces for all his life
A she-hare that doesn't stop laughing
With the spell of kisses   Such a record
I keep listening three whole days

The night train to Chicago
Let's take Train A
Blues that Lou Rawls sings
"Goin' to Chicago Blues"
We were blues too then
Of tomorrow
Ah if we think of tomorrow
"We gotta drink muddy water"
Ah Lou Rawls is always happy
When he sings
In a hustler suit on the street
But why does he say
"Stormy Monday"?

We arrived
On Friday
On Friday when an eagle was flying
At the womb-station
Huge, dirty and old
In the underground where Ma was waiting

How many times do you say
We should jump into bed and love?
My darling America
Nobody now says
A gentle American
Silently they know
He is an ex-star in Hollywood
Rich, young and handsome
Now slightly losing his charms
Suffering from three kinds of cancer
But such a word as gentle
Is nowadays used only for hippies

Homosexual love
Give me your panties
With chastity and a handsome youth in it
Send it by express
To that George's shop on Buggery Street No. 10
Roses easily perish as well as art
And soon become refined in taste
Like those cheese-pies

Madame Blanche sleeps well
For education art galleries and museums
Because children enjoy themselves

Don't cry
You must grow big and strong
Dancing, holding
Eating, quarreling
Making love, traveling
Boxing, walking

Sleeping they cried
As the two
Had just opened the lid of love
They didn't know how to drink
It's a long way to the damn honey taste
How many tens of years more
O America, my darling
Before you become a cook of honey in Hell
I don't know you
Is your name America, you who are here?
No
You are a bright anonymity
My private America
Not canned but fresh in taste and smell
Soul food
Crossing trifling time together
Soul time, darling
Be careful with snakes   and then
A kiss good night

Atsumi

KORA RUMIKO 1932–

Born in Tokyo. She attended Keio University and Tokyo College of Fine Arts. She also travelled to Europe through Southeast Asia, and studied for one year in Paris, mainly poetry. She won the Mr. H. Prize, and has published the essays, *The Words of Things. The Pupil and the Bird* was published in 1958.

THE TREE

Within a tree there is a tree which does not yet exist.
Now its twigs tremble in the wind.

Within a blue sky there is a blue sky which does not yet exist.
Now a bird cuts across its horizon.

Within a body there is a body which does not yet exist.
Now its sanctuary accumulates fresh blood.

Within a city there is a city which does not yet exist.
Now its plazas sway before me.

Kora

AWAKENING

After objects jostled past me,
trees turned their leaves
and shut me off from the world.

Out of this emptiness,
I touch the hot texture of a cheek;
a naked arm; dark rocks lying everywhere under the earth.

(I escaped the void
and went along the easy curves of leaves in darkness
towards the border
because you were there;
because you were not there.)

In an atmosphere of heated matter,
I search under my eyelids for a speed
faster than dust falls at dawn.

When clear morning light
opens my eyes from inside,
a crisis also awakens.
My hands mix the unknown breath of objects
with the earth's morning they can't see.

Kora

AUTUMN

It is now autumn in the universe.
A young girl who attempted suicide
recovers, knowing she can leave her family.
A man from across the sea
talks about your isolation more clearly than you.
The lower leaves of a magnolia turn yellow
where sunlight slips through.
Eternity suddenly appears
in the lights of an oncoming bus.
One autumn day like this

the world rapidly shrinks,
and people living on distant deserts
become familiar.
Unexpectedly, you feel transparency invading your body through
    your tail,
and you quickly rise from your chair.
Your short rest is finished.
You are already in a new activity.

Kora

SHE

The azalea's white petals open
like the earth's dizziness.
A woman becomes invisible
in their combining odors.

Petals are scattered at her feet
with objects that were illusions.
They change into an ocean of dark vomit
and buoy her up.

Drifting on endless waves,
little by little she forgets
her home,
flower-words,
the ocean,
her wandering.

. . . between the petals of the sheets,
she awakens without a life history, without shame,
by the side of a man coming back to her.

Kora

THE MOON

I shoot, aiming at the moon,
and the moon laughs.
Her silver laughter
invites one hundred birds
from branches
sleeping in my spirit.

Kora

THE FRIEND

I felt light in my eyes.
The afternoon sun shattered in the hair of a girl running towards
    me.
A policeman wearing earphones smiled on a chair in front of his police
    box.
My friend, who once shared our aspirations,
worked in a deep green shadow in his studio;
telephone and ink bottle on his left, ashtray and pen rack on his
    right.
Green light coming through the tree
filled the air in the dry room.
Shall I continue or quit . . . ?
I was saying something
about the man I was living with.
What became of our aspirations?
Are they dead as pebbles?
The telephone rang like an alarm.
Unfinished letters for a poster
lay on his desk.

I looked at the needles of my watch.
"Continue!" he said.
His wife, born in the year of the ram,
poured coffee in blue cups.
His solid body
existed in this small pre-fab room.
"Continue . . ."
Once more the telephone rang.
I went to the door and saw the garden
where an old tree spread its heavy leaves.
I could sense an old person in the main house
whom I had heard died there.
The last dozen years flashed before me
between a face from the past
and this little-changed garden.
If I quit
would our aspirations live?

The reddening ginko trees
stand in rows, gathering dewy evening light.
Among these trees glowing like flame
the light became increasingly brilliant.
As I walked the heated pavement
snapping like popcorn,
suddenly, the light fragmented.

Kora

IWATA HIROSHI 1932–

Born in Hokkaido. He attended Tokyo
College of Foreign Languages, where his
major was Russian. He translated
Mayakovsky, Ehrenburg, and Solzhenit-
syn, and published a study, "Mayakov-
sky's Love." *Tyranny* was published in
1956.

SEASIDE EXPERIMENT

1

With the girls   I
High on the cliff look   down
To the sea.   A man steps
Naked from the sea.   Spring
            every spring
A blind man shudders
            out of the sea
Testicles dropping
            water drops.

We're at *Inamuragasaki*
            Kamakura
But at every beach I've ever known
    Kamaishi Abashiri Kure Kuju kuri
            one naked man
Arms spread   flung to the sun
            comes
            runs.

Look
How the wind ripples the hair on his legs
How his muscles flow
                    how dark are
Red his lips
The twisted fish hook tattooed
                    on his brow
On his shoulders a sea urchin.

    2
Hand in hand with these girls
                    crueller than myth
On a cliff sown with cones   I
    Wait for him   the man naked

Understand.
                    He is gentle.
                              Feet
Hair   palms elegant though scarred
By the nets   the twisting of the nets
                              back
Big enough to paint on. Gentle.
From *Hokkaido* to *Kyushu* nowhere
Will you find a man more gentle
                    more free

Islands   you   these   all islands
                    girls
Gathered in a net like islands
Once   for you   I tore off
My skin   to bind my poems.

But this man   this one running
Blind and elegant out of the sea
This one can sit in the yellow sand
Sit while we watch breathless
                    and count
Clockvoiced
Backward   from ten
To Zero.

Fitzsimmons

TYRANNY

   1
Under the cliff   air
Ran like water
Shadows were distinct in light
And fleece floated
The camera so perfectly focused
That the touch of fleece and the cool moss
Cool on the forehead
Crossed vision   spectrum in
Memory twisted like rainbow
Three men on three horses
Come softly this way
Soldiers
Franco's soldiers

A song   yes there was a song
Deep in the loudspeaker lustrous soprano
On off a song and
Suddenly birds leap high

Under the soaring cliff
Air smooth as unrolled film
Only hoofs
Come and go
Between our hearts and the screen
(enterar y callar)
Echoing
When the cold air enters our bodies
Spain at dawn
Disappears.

   2

Pure as a madman gone crazy
Obscene as a saint   thick
Beyond recall
Colder than crystal
Baffling as father to son
Son to father
More priceless often than eyes is
History

Bad conscience chooses a back road   always.
Is night's task
Ours
Merely to bet
Endlessly crouching
Shrinking
Flutter   patter   threading fears
Shadow light   shadow again?

Fumbling through a bushy hedge
Fingers and fingernails seek sounds
Jubilee Jubilay
Who was it?

A girl fallen innocently asleep
All over piano keys
Body ringing final consonance

Lines in my lower lip
Stains and freckles   holes
All over

   3

White paper. Paper white   bloodless. In a vast room of frosted
glass I stand naked. Naked lover and friends each sweats blue
juice bathed in a dizzy artificial light dragging faint shadow.

If at least our bodies were too transparent for them to see
the musicians behind the glass. Into the lightcapped roundroom
music from everywhere flows   in colourless scentless streams
condemning our girls

Seeming to fall they start to dance eyeless like jewels without
lips twinkle twinkling they dance Harlem Nocturne black voice
of no male no female black voice dull worn voice sings dizzy
darkness thickens but I am paper white no face burning red coals
no reconciliation with the dark torturers the grey glass that
stares shines in their busy sighs 'a blue tune'

   4

Dreams end in a rustle   audience
impatient for the curtain to rise
Rising with the tide small world   mine
Inflated to the limit

Fanfare

In clear consciousness
Trusting my sweat and blood to words

Against silence finally here
I say Tyranny
Tyranny comes

Silence
Orchestra long finished playing
Audience holds the breath
That one in the centre
Woman who reigns over all this
In whom the evanescent future waits
Singer   our singer
But she does not sing
Lo   her   dress   is   withered   she
Opens her mouth   closes it and
With a scream no one hears
Falls

Please   Silence   Calm down   Listen
Tyranny is coming   there it is
In daylight gentler than night into
A present dimmer than dream that
Sings the woman comes
And your voice dies
Her throat is more fragile than a whisper
Delicate ears hair always protected now
Given to the wind but unchanged when she sings
And your voice dies
Never sing to the sea never
To the sky
Swifter than speed
Tyranny comes to soil tree and water
Tremble before it
Aim at its eyes

Tyranny comes sings the woman
And your voice dies

Fitzsimmons

DAMN SONG

Morning   eight o'clock
Last night's dream
Seeps under the train door
Sings its song
"Want to sleep?
Hey.   Want to sleep?
Yes?   Or No?"
Damn song   Damn song
I want to sleep   can't
Can't sleep
    Difficult girl   wasted seed
    Sly mind and frozen love
    Square habits   sea urchin

Lunch break   an old love
In a bill collector's suit
Sings its song
"Want to forget?
Hey.   Want to forget?
Yes?   Or No?"
Damn song   Damn song
I want to forget   can't
Can't forget
    Difficult girl   wasted seed

Sly mind and frozen love
Square habits   sea urchin

Evening   six o'clock
Tomorrow's wind
Stretches dark gentle hands
Sings its song
"Want to dream?
Hey.   Want to dream?
Yes?   Or No?"
Damn song   Damn song
I want to dream   don't
Don't dream
    Difficult girl   wasted seed
    Sly mind and frozen love
    Square habits   sea urchin
    A sea urchin

Fitzsimmons

SATURDAY NIGHT DATE

   1
Phone call in late afternoon
sunny afternoon:
a girl   a date.

In the blue light of shop windows
seven o'clock   a scarlet coat
she sees me and smiles
            but
a wind   something like a wind
        swells between us.

Water trembles in the glass as
she drinks   shop talk   friend
talk   health   the rain   we
babble like birds then   silence
                    why?

    2

The thin tube of time is choked
with grime   you can puff
till your eyes pop   nothing
gets through.

Yet sometimes it's clear
then you blink surprise
back off   laugh   make
nervous parrot noises
cock an eyebrow to show
you can't be fooled   so
your ears ring
                    as the tube closes.

    3

The wind again   head wind
If I face east, it's from the east,
west   it shifts to the west
What   whose stubbornness is this?

We stare into the dark   strain
into the dark   there's no one there
no one to see   but if we both
close our eyes at once
                    the wind dies down.

It all started gaily enough
like a great electric sign

switching on   but what?
Streets at night   children
in the streets   soldiers in the
streets   Mobil Standard Oil.

What is it that darkens the stars?
Looms up between us and the sky?
What holds us both like whores
on the street? Shuffling whoreshapes?
               Mobil Standard Oil

Fitzsimmons

CALM SONNET

My weakness: lacking calmness.
Koto strings snap, pothooks break,
orange rice-gruel burns my lips,
a hundred policemen smash through my peritoneum.

Stinking water rises into man-shape,
the man whose waving arms threaten the sardine clouds.
But calm down. Stop reading comics.
Better spend some time smashing bean-curd castles.

What should I choose as a model of composure—
deposits for squid houses; down-payments on rags;
a gas man squatting in the corner of an ice-house?
I should freeze to the bone before saying,

"Shut up, old men. We don't get much money.
Think, you kids. Your work pays nothing."

Atsumi

MIKI TAKU 1935–

Born in Tokyo. He spent his childhood in Manchuria, and graduated from Waseda University, having majored in Russian literature. A writer of juvenile literature, he won the Mr. H. Prize. He was also an editor of a literary publishing house. *3 a.m. Tokyo* was published in 1966.

THE HOWLING MAN

When my family falls asleep
I feel like I'm floating on a dark sea of fire.
My stiffened body senses
an enormous silence squatting here,
as if I touched flame, rhinoceros, iron.
Now, hidden in my body;
someone blowing a trumpet with broken valves
and a tenor singing out of key
watch cold towns in the bluest darkness
and a low range of overlapping mountains.
A man hovers around, a shadow howling
like a wild beast, as if
to destroy these dread hours.
That sad sound is already familiar to me
in Oriental towns, outside fenced-in hospitals, in dimly-lit
    markets.
The man knows the world of bated breath,

the world that thrusts a knife towards the tightened bowstring.
And he drifts from place to place
crying *hooo hooo*.

Whang

ESCAPE FROM THE CITY

I kept walking until the city frayed.
Eyes shut, I felt split
by my surrender to the back of a dense odor.
A huge, curving, high-speed road glistened smoothly.
Hidden here and there
were deep, black, reedy swamps holding round waters,
all of them pocks of bombs.
I continued along through luxuriant buttercups,
enduring the dazzling light: my sore throat exposed
to winter winds.
Thick feet in fashionable stockings
moved through the narrow swamps, and lay sideways,
and cramped toes kicked the air.
I heard a conspicuously high moan.
Though I could see no form,
someone like me must have been there.
The isolated swamps I had stumbled across
were filled with abundant signs of animals.
A tinfoil chocolate wrapper rustled under a shoe-sole.
Bamboo grass sprang back, suddenly slashing my palms.
Mud stuffed up my shoe-lace holes.
I saw swamp-plants with joints as large as a giant bamboo's,

their long leaves swaying heavily; their sharp points
scratching the white sky.
Several white eddies twirled.
In an unzipped jump-suit, I looked back at the tilted, distant city
where I had cast my life,
and I could see a tall, steel antenna
aiming at my quickly aging body.
Am I not free even after coming this far?
I abandoned everything—
everything!—to turn back into a fighting beast.
A wind passed over the waving bamboo.
If I were unable to move, my testicles would cringe.
I continued,
my calves soaked with the stench of reed sap.
It awakened an excitement in me,
a pressing dizziness
distorting my field of vision
as if I had smelled chestnut pollen.
My sight curved and widened.
Aa!
Released! I rolled around cutting through the wind
but could not get up.
As I lay motionless, little by little
my surroundings brightened
revealing their original forms and colors.
Raising my body, I felt the coldness of my mud-soaked skin,
but I burned so that I could hear nothing.
Again, the swamp opened before me.
There was a clear sign that my girl had been waiting there for some
     time.
A familiar, trembling voice, like a wild duck shot on the wing,
rushed across the sky.

No longer any need to walk,
I crawled along
answering in a lover's voice.
The factory whistle, devoured by the winds,
blew distorted tones across the entire swamp.

Whang

ADOLESCENT THOUGHT

one morning   I lay awake in bed
and could clearly see the quiet lines of a procession
I lay in a lifeless bed soaked with night sweats
like a horse in sickness   limbs outstretched
tormented by nightmares
and sad crying
television was a fresh stimulus
and to sleepy ears   the landlady's lecture
on the fate of a bad law
was refreshing
kicking off dreams about a horse-cart   a tuxedo   a duel with a
      noble English writer
I watched a school uniform and the print by Klee on the wall
and thought about today's work . . .
a real morning pasted obliquely   deep underground
morning now wrapped in mist   in cold sweat
I want to live in the real morning
modest wishes
drive me to work
Yes!   we are neither horses
nor stable hands nor owners
we're saplings unafraid of axes

a young Birnham Wood moving freely
lying awake I can see it
the other side of my bed is dank with night sweat
the insides of my body are not fully mature
they're filled with pointed adolescent thoughts
like large-mesh hair nets
thoughts that can't contain anything
but no use crying over spilled milk
from here   thoughts mature
they're a sponge with body-heat   an organism
that can expand or shrink
look!   my *organism* demands words   words
that can be transferred to anybody
move from a hot body to a cold body
new words making themselves understood everywhere
in a quiet demonstration   in heated conference
in exhausting work   in cold laboratories
words like cooked rice that comrades
sharing work in order to capture the morning   can understand
strange signs   hard and easy to understand
as familiar as the taste of dried mackerel
or vegetables seasoned with rice-bran

when I get up   the vision is gone
the landlady scares me   demanding rent
now don't be put off
a thought unable to resist drudgery is useless
after I get up   I should not slight the landlady
so that I can continue to hear clearly
the footsteps of the procession   the shouts of men
wheels creaking and horses' neighs
in order to talk about struggle in a kind way

and happiness in clumsy tones
I will prize this very morning
and tell the landlady
"It's not just because of hard times.
I'll pay you as quick as I can."

Whang

MANAGED DAYS

At intervals in the slaughter
acquaintances were born one by one,
and they doze, crouching in a crucible.
Cobblers sew imaginary shoes, one after another;
drivers kick holes in their covers instead of kicking accelerators;
nights criss-crossed with terror pile up.
We fear we are going, bit by bit, away from our loved ones.
All of us laugh, and shake hands, and pat shoulders
a little too often;
all of us shake our heads trying not to think,
and cry as we fall asleep, and keep running until daybreak;
keep going on and on . . .
promises cramming our ventilator-equipped cerebrums,
toward a cold and harmonious heaven.

Compared to any of these disturbed days,
I know little about how my wife and sister,
who stretch strings of hope from this electrical appliance to that,
where "tsk-tsk" and sighs can be heard
above the incessant noise of scrubbrushes on tables,
and what wells up from these sounds
is more foreign to him

standing behind the door with boots in his hands
than any events of these disturbed days.
He is the cause of it all; he is their fate.
I no longer know how to share gestures
with close friends, familiar
yet vague, like old films;
nor share the feeling of hunger forced under our English coats.
I part. I trudge down steps to the subway.

Whang

GENEALOGY

The night I turned up in this world
Mama was incoherent with joy.
Papa, in a flurry, ran to the pawn shop,
and then to wake up the *sake* shop keeper.
After guzzling the wine,
he tied his sweat band really tight
and began working himself to death. In fact, he died.
After his death Mama worked hard,
grinding her widow's teeth.
Keep going! I entered a university in Tokyo
and finally, she made me graduate.
Mama, born in the year of the fire-horse, the pretty girl
who captivated Papa, at sixty is fat
but still full of energy.
Well now, I just had a daughter
and my wife was incoherent with joy.
In a flurry, I ran to the pawn shop,
and then to wake up the *sake* shop keeper.

Whang

CALCULATION

"Where is the joy
to equalize our misery?"
asked my melancholy friend.
"My feeling of losing my child
and your feeling of finding your child
do not balance.
The feeling of the whipped
and the feeling of the whipper
do not balance.
However, our universe is governed by the conservation of energy.
When you think about it, surely we're balanced by a nebula
    somewhere,"
he said, melancholily.

Whang

TOMIOKA TAEKO 1935–

Born in Osaka. She graduated from Osaka College of Women, with a major in English literature. She won the Mr. H. Prize, and published the essays, *Nihon, Nihonjin* (Japan, Japanese). Recently, she has turned to writing short stories. *Return Call* was published in 1956.

BETWEEN

There are two sorrows to be proud of

After slamming the door of the room behind me
After slamming the door
Of the entrance of the house behind me
And out on the street visibility zero because of
      the rain of the rainy season
When the day begins
Which way shall I go
What shall I do
To neither prospect
Am I friend or enemy
Who can I ask about
This concrete question
I hate war and
Am no pacifist
The effort only to keep my eyes open
The sorrow that I can make only that effort

There are two sorrows to be proud of

I am with you
I don't understand you
Therefore I understand that you are
Therefore I understand that I am
The sorrow that I do not understand you
The sorrow that you are what you are

Sato

LET ME TELL YOU ABOUT MYSELF

Because both Dad and Mom
Even the old midwife
In fact every single predictor
Bet that I'd be a boy
I tore out of the placenta determinedly a girl

Then
Because everybody regretted it
I became a boy
Then
Because everybody praised it
I became a girl
Then
Because everybody bullied me
I became a boy

When I came of age
Because my sweetheart was a boy
I had to be a girl
Then
Because everybody except my sweetheart

Talked about how I became a girl
I became a boy to everybody
Except to my sweetheart
Because I regretted being special to my sweetheart
I became a boy
Then because he said he wouldn't sleep with me
I became a girl

Meanwhile several centuries came to pass
This time
The poor caused a bloody revolution
And were being bossed around by a slice of bread
Therefore I became a medieval church
Saying love is the thing
I visited back alleys
Distributed old clothes and lumps of bread

Meanwhile several centuries came to pass
This time
God's land had come
And the rich and poor were great friends
So I hopped on a private helicopter
And scattered agitation leaflets

Meanwhile several centuries came to pass
This time
The bloody revolutionaries
Were kneeling before a rusted cross
I saw a fire of order in the disorder
So in the pub and in the den
Byron   Musset
Villon   Baudelaire
Hemingway   girls in black pants

And I played cards   drank
Talked nostalgically
About things like the libertines peculiar to the
Country in the East called Japan
And mainly
Made fun of things like
Simultaneity of love

Because both Dad and Mom
Even the old midwife
In fact everybody said I was a child prodigy
I was a cretin
Because everybody said I was a fool
I became an intellectual and set up a residence somewhere behind
I didn't know what to do with my energy

When the rumor became widespread
That I was an intellectual somewhere behind
I began to walk out in the front
The walk I walked
Was the same as my Dad and Mom's
I the pervert was confused
Was tormented for my reputation was at stake
And so
I became a good solid girl
I became a boy to my sweetheart
And wouldn't allow him to complain

Sato

LIVING TOGETHER

You'll make tea
I'll make toast
While we do things like this
Maybe early in the evening
A friend may notice the rising moon dyed scarlet
And maybe feel like visiting us
But that will be the last time he comes
We'll shut all the doors   lock them
Make tea   make toast
Talk as usual about how
Sooner or later
There will be a time you bury me
I bury you in the garden
And go out as usual to hunt for food
There will be a time you bury me
Or I bury you in the garden
The one left sipping tea
Then for the first time one will refuse fiction
Your freedom too
Was no better than a fool's story

Sato

WHAT COLOR WAS THE SKY

For example you see this:
on your way to buy morning bread
a young man leaning
against a sunny fence

was taking off his kimono.
What did you say
in a voice like French?
What did you say
in the animal language?
The wet cough of
a large-headed woman
in men's wooden clogs
frightened you so much
you forgot your greetings.
And you turned back
looking like a plant
picking up
the overturned syllables.
Perhaps you didn't have to die
on your way back
because of that.

Sato

HOW ARE YOU

How shall I put it?
It isn't that you do it with grace.
It's very simple
in fact, quite exhilarating
except
you better clip your nails shorter.
Everyone likes you
the moment you are seen.
There isn't an exception,

Tomioka • 227

you are liked by everyone.
You are trusted,
no matter what you do
you make them feel good.
At your age
you no longer have
anyone to betray,
anyone to rebel against,
you can't even dupe yourself.
You have nothing to talk about,
you can spend your whole day
plucking the nails of the cat.
But today too you've written to someone.
Today too you've washed your hands and feet.
Today too you put sugar in the coffee.
Today too you awoke in the morning.
Today too you left your bed.

Ah yes and
today too
you had an apple for a snack.
And dangling your Michaelangelo phallus
and angel breasts
you walked about a bit
and for a night snack
you sipped oyster stew.
Like a westerner
you tried to roar.
Like a Chinaman
you tried to meditate.
For all this you were there
after taking off your meaning

and your coat,
a tooth pick stuck in your mouth.
At any time indeed
you'll be there
drinking gin
eating locusts' legs.

Sato

PLEASE SAY SOMETHING

To a man eating a pear
you pose a question
like why the hell
he's turning on
and off the light
only when
you're sitting like an insect
on a chair
in the dark of
an autumn house
when revenge and such shit
doesn't count.
Which reminds us   doesn't it
how a nine year old girl
took off her kimono
yesterday
better than her mom does.
Then   remember
the insect like a golden green
grass ball creeping up

the outstretched arm.
Oh I know   all of
these stories sound too good
to believe   right.
Have a pancake
or something
for a night snack
and give it good thought
OK?

Sato

MARRY ME PLEASE

I didn't go anywhere
but cut down all the trees
in the backyard
and weeded all the grass
around them.
They bore children,
the children went to war
and when they returned
the children bore children.
The children flood the land
and females can only take hot baths.
It will soon be over.
Perhaps grass will begin to grow.
Man will die among the grass.

Sato

CHAIRS

I greeted the human being.
At any time
I have nothing to say.
I remember seeing
a photo of a beach
where many
round wicker chairs
are arranged.
Inside those shell-like chairs
I'll greet again.
About the chairs
there was nothing more
to be said.
You will put your hand
where the space ends
and look around.
Our short
trips have no sound
at any time.
Either one of us
may weep
in the air.
The chairs are
always put
back to back.
How light we are.
Don't hug me
so intimately
will you.

Sato

Tomioka • 231

THE GIRLFRIEND

My neighbor
The mistress recites a sutra
A little past noon
I saw an animal like a donkey
Pass below the window
I saw it through the opening in the curtains
Always through the opening in the curtains
A woman comes to see me
But today she hasn't come yet
Wearing a georgette Annamese dress
The line of her hip attractive to men
She promised to come
Today she hasn't come yet
Today she may have died
The other day
When I traveled with her
At a country antique shop
She wanted an old wood engraving
From Germany or some such place
At a country inn
For the first time with my fingers
I could mess up
The mass of her hair
Like Brigitte Bardot's
We danced
For a long time
Scarlet cheek to cheek
We danced a Viennese waltz
Her transparency
Her optimistic poesy

Occasionally spills like beads of sweat
Which I would take for tears
She does not come today
Like my neighbor the mistress
Though still midday
I pray aloud
She did not promise
That she would not come
You are gone
You who are gone

Sato

GREETINGS

Because you were embarrassed
you were about to talk.
Your father has left to die
and your mother will die on her way home.
Take me some place.
Lately you have often failed
to be an old man.
So you imitated a Chinese poet
and said simply:
I regret I couldn't drink as much as I wanted.

Sato

OSADA HIROSHI 1939–

Born in Fukushima City, Northern Japan. He graduated from Waseda University, having majored in German literature, and writes essays and dramas. He published the essays, *Revolution in Lyrics*, and others. He was a member of The University of Iowa International Writing Program, 1971–72. *We, the Fresh Traveller* was published in 1965.

MY POETRY

Today I tried to write a poem
but couldn't write a line.
Just what did I mean to write on?
Fat souls?
Supple justice?
No; love that runs like a rabbit?
What should I have written on?
How can there be silence without malice?
Poetry sure isn't a craft or *originalité*.
The mind isn't a bank. I want to
tie my poetry to some threatening hope.
That poetry defies death's large hands.
As a homosexual honestly loathes licentiousness,
I want to knock out my existence with pointed hatred.
Stupid-ass-you-son-of-a-bitch!
View-view-reviews-shit-on-you!
I shout; birds, soldiers, pianists shout!
I do not accept such stuff as exterritoriality of sensibilities.

234 •

But, I, a bared emotion!
Recognize my helplessness and sorrow.
And
bear the remarkable lack of
the first line of our time.

Lento

THE PHANTOM CLASS

In a place that belongs to no one
we work all day
while genuine hunger mews like a kitten
under death's surveillance.

There'll be no despair if there's no cruel future.
Our long day is, like a white roll of toilet paper,
a sequel to the nightmare of
the concentration camp.

When did we become aphasics
like dignified pets
having tamed our sense of anger
wondering only how we ought to die?

Weren't we members of the phantom class?
We have refused to die defeated
like gentle Ophelia
among tender wheat ears and cornflowers?

Lento

I do not know the weight of polished guns
nor the roar of strafing.
I do not know the bitter glimmer of planes that
drew the image of death to the blue's far end;
nor do I know the chill of the soldier of mist
who lay with his fatigued feet stuck in the heated sea.
In the eyes of people who speak of these
there is always a strange gleam.
That makes me uneasy.
But today
our love turned it aside.
                    I found out afterwards
it was wrong to assume when we met for the first time,
that we would understand each other.
When the dusk sneaks up with its front paws close together,
slowly down the cobblestones by the
filthy creek where the damp smell of stale oil crawls,
we walk, the two of us, arm in arm,
carrying in a handful the day's fatigue.
What we share at that time
without knowing, through faint warmth,
is a part of our hearts where we try to
console each other.
(How much more can we do?)

This is not a matter of believing or not believing,
nor a matter of doing this when we can't do that.
I will live in spite of death's malice.
To live is our task.
Once in a while I say

without even blinking,
"I will garnish your hair
with a fragrant flower.
Give me in return a tender kiss."
Is this a sign of tenderness?
or of the hollowness of this age?

But this is us. We've got to act out
the fate that chose us.
No one can pick another time, another act.
Toward the yet-unnamed world hanging above our lips,
we shout or stay silent, slowly stepping forward
as our own weight shifts until
it finally becomes an act,
however unsightly it may be.
Throughout history, which heats and sharpens itself,
and through its deep meaning
on this spot
we can live only with our warm trembling hearts.

    Our love fosters a process.
    Or, the process brings on love itself.

To continue, to continue!
We cuddle together in our only continuation
romping like kittens.

Lento

We left for nowhere.
We did not clap our hands, we did not know
the sublimity of mature death.

We were made of coldness.
We despised the metaphor of the dawn
and were starved like scrawny geese.

History seemed like rumors.
Like a hockey player who missed a goal
we stood absently in our opponent's field.

We talked impatiently, did things hastily.
Fads were fashionable, factions conspired.
Rhetoric always cancelled out sophism.

Where no one could see, someone was
twining together apostasy and pain.
He was pilfering life like petty cash.

In other words, we were popular with despair.
In other words, we happily took neighborhoods for the world.
We'd seen neither revolution nor an African baboon.

So, we have been here.
There was nothing else.
If we grow older, we grow older as we stand.

Nobody left for anywhere.
Nope, nobody even raised his eyebrow.
Whether to laugh or cry, nobody opened up.

Lento

I SHOUTED

In a park inside the park
swinging the swing inside the swing
I saw the things around me shift:
the cleaner's became two then three
the confectioner's got filled with greens
the barber's began to spin like a three colored flag
the trike floated over the roofs
far away in the cloud's distance
the strawberry shortcake glittered like a dinosaur.
Swell, no problem.
I am a genius magician. Don't you know that?
Then I proudly ordered Mischa, the bear,
"Sing Mary Poppins."
"Make faces."
But Mischa said he wouldn't like that,
shook his head three, five times.
That was the end. The April circus must break up.
Rats, I failed.
I jumped down the wind, and ran.
What shall I become now? I ran and ran.
Pearlworts, Rhododendron, hedges and all ran with me.
I ran and fell, fell and ran and I made up my mind.
I won't become anything!
I will be someone who doesn't become anything!
Stomping, I shouted tearfully.

Lento

A LIFE OF FIGHTING

Go croak, tower!
Go croak, ivory ear!

Croak, all pacts and courts,
charities and chatty reporters.

Without humbug what celebration
do we have?

Let us not live
to count up the drenched defeats

Do not live, unconcerned, in fear
Do not live, hanging your tongue out with the dogs.

Go croak, tower
Go croak, ivory ear

Go to hell
There's no time limit to any cases

Do not chat hand in hand
Do not chatter with metaphors

we've got to work, and work
The thing is, how much rejection we stand

Crying and babbling
how can we build our dream land

Go croak, tower
Go croak ivory ear

Go to hell, all of you
beautiful "ladies and gentlemen" made of dust.

Lento

JAILHOUSE ROCK

An onion next to a soul;
plugs in the ears of all the living.
Nowadays scads of scarecrows scatter.

Birds fall out of trees; turtles tumble over,
dogs chase their own tails.
Nowadays happiness sleeps with frustration.

How naive,
what a gloomy back-stabbing age.
Nowadays we're squatting in saliva.

There're no white teeth to bite into a fruit's flesh.
There's no one who dies knowing the necessary pain.
Nowadays a dream is like a dose of powder medicine.

Those who don't know don't want to know more.
Those who don't see won't even look.
Nowadays none look at things other than what they see.

How naive,
what a gloomy back-stabbing age.
Nowadays we only know what we want to know like a narrow
    specialist.

All the lies only are rusing
from precocity to maturity; they rush like lawmakers.
Nowadays the wrong grow older uprightly.

But unconvicted prisoners don't forget
us the outsiders who have neglected those absent,
us who forget about them.

How naive,
what a gloomy back-stabbing age.
We are shouting, "We're ready!" running away from the it.

But remember, we haven't been forgiven even once.
The outside world is just the outside of the jailhouse.
Nowadays our suburb is the jailhouse itself.

Lento

BLUE BLUES
TO REMEMBER NOT TO REMEMBER

My gentle one,
spread your thighs wide—
so our child, who died unborn
when still soft as a snow peach
covered with downs of death, can return
into its bloody tent of hunger and shadow.
"Listen, can you hear?"
Among the folds of your flesh
that smell of strong salt
the bones of the baby, who had yet no shape,
scatter into pieces
ringing like the distant breeze . . .

Do not smile like that, like a mirror,
my gentle one, innocent murderer.
I swear hundreds of times that
I really love you, but
what can we do about our helplessness and
this pitiful end of a life

that dissolved like a drop of warm water
in the crimson darkness of your womb?

Hide your tears in your lashes, your groans in your throat.
and your timid love in your defiant silence!
Beside your trembling tender armpit,
I suddenly realize we know what it is to be old.
Fatigued like a captive ox,
my gum line smeared with dark blood,
my gentle one,
I hold your breasts tight
in the dark tattered sunbeams
at your red fear-wrought strawberry patch.

My gentle one,
spread your thighs wide!
Our intense pain has centered on
a stroller that always collapses at dawn.
Have we been falling a long time
like snowflakes that sparkle and dissolve
in a distant summer's day?
Now the fleshy glow calmed,
with amniotic words I seek
a specter of you, a shroud,
on the pious visage of the night.
Sledding like sex splashing through seasons
stooping over like a dog
I give a kiss
to your death colored pubic hair
to the young wheat ears cropped before harvest time,
to the silence that quietly resembles enmity.

Can we still do it?
Can we embrace friendship just as
we hold a bunch of full-bloomed anemones?
My mysterious accomplice, this thirst like sin!
Our truth and cowardice are all just one sorrow?
Deep down in the dazzling emptiness in your arms
you are today the mother whom you desecrate,
and to the father in me you are the only enemy.
"Come, open your fists and warm your
cold cheeks with your palms."
On my flat chest we artlessly tangle
our fingers, as if praying, and we weep.
We are like two grains of sand heated on the surf.

My gentle one,
we could never betray hope in any way, so
let us now sleep until we violently awake
at the other end of this screaming darkness
· · · · ·

Ah, to us
parting always comes without warning!

Lento

REFUSAL TO TELL

Inside your mouth today
the taste of tepid blood spreads. It is
the stuff called your freedom. Yesterday
the police beat you up.

Inside your ears today
hundreds of mutes' screams break out. It is
the stuff called your defeat. Yesterday
the police beat you up.

You are your rage, your dream
you told them you have no such thing as a name.
Sadly shaking his head, saying it is a lie, yesterday
a policeman beat you up.

You don't own much:
an unhappiness that runs
threading its way between madness and madness,
your shy spineless eternal revolution, and

words! your words, like those an orphan speaks to another,
those the stutterer starts babbling—the words, that's all.
Sadly shaking his head, saying it's a lie, yesterday
a policeman beat you up.

Lento

WHAT THE YOUNG CANADIAN INDIAN SAID

We aren't the children of the golden age.
We cannot live chasing Buffalo.

Wild berries, horses and shadows disappeared.
No maps show our country.

The world was simple a long time ago.
The River Saskatchewan, Lake Winnipeg—that was all.

It was the time of good youths.
One day it all turned to dust, as did the prairies.

Do not say you miss what's lost.
It is coming to crush me with its unseen weight.

If there's a train bound for Heaven
on the Canadian National Railway I'll take it sometime.

Now I hold my knees and sit in the doorway.
It's a long time from morning till night. Life is short.

Fear is my enemy.
I don't see reconciliation as wisdom.

Alcohol can't remove stains on the soul.
Not a prayer, but fire; give me instead a cold fire.

Lento

A POEM FOR A LULLABY

I sleep sitting right on the floor.
With my arms curved like hooks, with my knees bent,
still my feet stick out of my dream.

In this posture I bear the weight of darkness.
With my eyes open, with my mouth shut, looking up at the ceiling
of time I stare at errors that seem correct.

I pick a hundred hopes in a day, despair one thousand times,
grab the pillow full of chaff as if it were a warm heart
and I sleep
then I hear from somewhere unbelievably far
a hunchbacked girl hastily whisper to a suspicious lone assassin.

"We were born in the same country. Our country is Melancholia,
the dark place between Transylvania and Lithuania:
the Republic where all the people had their jaws shaved off.

"Yes, that is the only country
a lonely soldier returns to. He keeps blowing
his little bugle, weeping."

Then I sink into what wells up in myself
and sleep with my eyes stubbornly shut;
what can I see when my eyes are closed, I believe.

Something common but nobody has seen it
like fireworks in the winter sky,
love that arises surprisingly near

agony sharp as salt:
all these I call to my mind, holding my breath,
as if writing an alphabet on the desk with beer froth.

And finally I recall a cat I buried in our yard some time ago.
Images of its white teeth and a gobbet of rotting flesh.
I clutch at a sleep I can not sleep.

Lento

I MUST PAY MY DEBT

I grab words with their sharp ends down.
This is my way.
Just as a fish vendor grabs
a spearfish by its tail in the evening sun.

I grab a word like an antique dagger.
Mother once showed me how to hold it
saying we can die any time if only
we have courage enough to cut open our chests.

To me, the dagger looked
like a freshly cut white lily.
The pained flower sent forth its fragrance.
And

Mother failed to kill herself.
From the puddle of unbelievably thin blood
her tender mad eyes looked up at me:
What shall I do with this backstabbed poverty?

The world is made of beautiful deadly weapons:
this was the first thing I learned
from the age. That was the only word
my mother taught me.

So, I live grabbing words
with their sharp ends down
among enemies who formed me.
The misery is my debt; I must pay off my debt.

Lento

GOZO YOSHIMASU 1939–

Born in Tokyo. He graduated from Keio University, with a major in Japanese literature. He was a member of the University of Iowa International Writing Program, 1970–71. *Departure* was published in 1964.

MAD IN THE MORNING

I shout the first line of my poem
I write the first line
A carving knife stands up madly in the morning
These are my rights!

The glow of morning or a woman's breasts are not always beautiful
Beauty is not always first
All music is a lie!
Ah! First of all, let's close all the petals and fall down to the earth!

This morning, September 24, 1966
I wrote a letter to my dearest friend
About original sin
About the perfect crime and the method of destroying intelligence

Ah!
What a drop of water rolling on my pale pink palm!
The woman's breasts are reflected in a coffee saucer!
Oh! I can't fall down!
Though I ran rapidly over the edge of the sword, the world has not
    disappeared!

Yoshida

BURNING

The golden sword looks directly at the sun
Ah!
The pear blossom reflected on a fixed star!

The wind blows
In an Asian region
The soul is a wheel speeding on clouds

My will
Is to become blind
    to become sun and apple
    and not to become like them
    to become woman's breast, sun, apple, sheet of paper,
        pen, ink, and dream!
    To become weird music. And that's all.

Tonight, you
In a sports-car
A star shooting at you from the front
Can you tattoo it on your face? You!

Yoshida

MY LOVE, A FIRE

Tonight I felt like an ancient architect
Ah
The Stars and Stripes suits the night sky
Again, my green hunting for words begins
I
Kill gold with gold

I bring all lies closer to lies
I'm burning up, my love, a fire!
How
I ignore myself
Tonight again
Drawing a long red line of alcohol like an arch
Seven miles in the night's path
I carved the face of the universe
A glance!
The sharp-toothed wheel rolls over my eyeballs
Now
Parting from my dearest friend
Tonight I feel like a corpse   '
So now
I take out my hidden poems from a drawer
And read them out
    (I am a god)
    (Deep in my thought)
    (A transparent corpse lies under the duckweed)
    (I am sad)
I don't understand
Is there any secret metamorphosis in this poem?
These are the notes for a loveletter perhaps never to be written
Ah
The Stars and Stripes suits the night sky
I am a madman on the roof
I support the heavenly bodies in a roofy sense
I make love, my love, a fire in the sky above
A picture of hell
Long hair caressed by flames like a tree
Night and day, the voice of the stars taken by a black lens
And

Again
I'm looking for my love, a fire
Rolling rapidly
A bloody
Head just cut off!
Waving goodbye to the night sky!

Yoshida

THE ANCIENT CASTLE IN THE AIR

That silver
Ancient Castle in the Air on which the snow lies deep
The silver
Ancient Castle in the Air on which the snow lies deep
Ah
The snow falls and falls
The snow falls and
A white lover is coming
Ah, what a supernatural
Silver
Large rock, covered by snow, insanity attacking the nucleus,
    thick silver snow, bloodthirstiness closing in
    on the brain, snow on the sense organs, each
    frozen hard, oh, the row of big white columns beginning to
        turn
    into a mystery! look all corpses suddenly shine
    crimson!
The snow lies on the Ancient Castle in the Air
Down the European cliff, the snow lies deep, the silver haired
Silver

White horse is moving
The horse fades into its ghost, the white horse is moving
Slowly, toward the super-camera slowly
Slowly the music is beginning to flow
The melody is slowly
Beginning to flow
The silver white horse passes under the tower, the silver
    doll on its back, which becomes a non-existing symbol
    going around the sense organs, giving a sign, then
    quietly, the horse begins to run like a gust of wind!
Chandelier
Chandelier
Where do you burn your white flame!
White horse! Break the circle, break it through
White horse, white horse
Riding over the cosmos
O, the silver
White horse
The 4th of January, 1970
Moving
In this haunted room of Shimokitazawa
The snow lies deep
I was suspended from the ceiling by a silver string, then thrown
    with a big crash!
Ah, chandelier
Whatever I become, a phantom or archfiend or shooting star,
            flying up from the haunted room, I will use
            magic, I will metamorphose into the snow,
            appear from the edge of a big lens!
The white horse is a white horse, it runs fast
White is white: there is the whole authority of words!
The silver, the silver

White horse, white horse
Ah, the Ancient Castle in the Air sank in the ocean, and
Gave up the gravitation of the Alps
In the north the dark room is burning with furious flames
The sun passes by the Book of Purgatory
Central Asia is gazing at it with terrible eyes
Burn, blue-black haired Africa
Thinking of the comet dreaming in the center of metal
Ah, lamp in the brain the great dictionary purifying the pure white!
The silver
Ancient castle in the Air on which the snow lies
The silver
Ancient Castle in the Air on which the snow lies
Can I love, can I love, can I love, can I kill,
      can I kill, can I kill, the silver white horse of the
      Revelations!
The keel always follows ghosts, and the ocean is a terrible
      bed, and when the big ship thrusts out from the sea like
      a leaning tower, the cities do the same! the Tower of
      Babel too, all focusing on shapes of house, ah, a
      house is also an Ancient Castle in the Air!
History and genitals, a terrible connection
What a custom, decorating with a pattern of time
The century of the phoenix, it is an ill omen!
Thinking of the corpse of a beauty
I sing the old song from Manyoshu
      "I feel sad the grass root on the shore, once touched
      by the Prince of Kume, has withered."
Ah, once touched
Dreaming of the Ancient Castle in the Air
Dreaming of the Ancient Castle in the Air
I sing today's solitary

Songs
The silver, white horse, my departed soul
Words fall like the snow, run through the snow, slide, race on, and
Enter true existence
Ah
I write Mako in the sky
I write a thousand lines of Mako
A thousand poetical lines are like masturbation!
I write Mako in the sky
I write a thousand lines of Mako
Mako-no, Midori-no, Mako-no, Midori-no,
    Mako-no, Midori-no, Mako-no, Midori-no, "once touched"
The pure white lover metamorphoses into Mako!
Sits straight like a corpse, touching the line of a man's name!
Now
The magic words appear in the name of an actress!
Surroundings, the world, the phony world surrounds
Mako-no, Midori-no, Mako-no, Midori-no, Mako-no, Midori-no
Mako-no, Midori-no, Mako-no, Midori-no, Mako-no, Midori-no
I write a line, then I scream, I write a line, then I scream,
    Mako, Magician!
Mako, Magician, go to the terrible dark mountain ridges
The snow falls, the snow falls
In the snow
Run fast to the Ancient Castle in the Air, climb up straight
The line of a man's name is the magic power, and forms super-
    word possessing great destructive powers!   man's name is
    equal to matter, too, crossing history, and the
    keel progresses with splashes of blood, look, look at the
    epitaph, look at the epitaph, one thousand
    Buddhist stupas spring up above the horizon, and sing
    a chorus!

The snow falls, the snow falls
In the snow
Dreaming of the Ancient Castle in the Air
Dreaming of a corpse
I walk in the shade of my illusion!
Moreover
Easily
I write a thousand lines of Mako
I write a thousand lines of Mako
Again
Giving up the gravitation of the Alps
I will offer my life
In the sky, in the coffin, the corpses breathe, the super-words
    breathe
Moreover the corpses dream and the spurting white flames
Yesterday, the black hair, chandelier
Yesterday, the black hair, chandelier
The snow lies deep
The snow lies deep
The silver
Ancient Castle in the Air
The snow lies deep
The snow lies deep
The silver
Ancient Castle in the Air
Seeking for a phantom, my love, a fire, seeking for the
    corpse, then becoming a huge structural power!   you, the
    tree, witness with your eyes this shadow freezing on the
    horse and running fast, you, the tree, your collapse is
    equal to the destruction of the world, defend the line of a
    man's name, commit murder!   the terrible flood of swords!
    The vast forest with white eyes!

Moreover
The snow lies deep
The snow lies deep
The Ancient Castle in the Air

Yoshida

THE FALLING OBJECT

Plotting to destroy words within my spirit
Brandishing a cluster of wisteria blossoms
Whipping the body of a woman hiding in the dark
The existence of the only king of gold!
Also
It might be said like this
The irreplaceable distrust found by my life
The existence of the question, "Where does the desert
    begin?" . . .
O, the tower of the brain projecting the old instincts!
Silence is impossible
Nonsilence is impossible
Only the winding of a venomous snake crushing unhappiness to
    pieces
On the road far away
Rising up becoming a burning rope

Ah
"The justice of a fountain"—Don't intrude!
Let's exchange the promise, with anybody
But the absolute avoidance. Is this my fate
Building words in a fertile rice field?
O, cannon!

Cashbook
Words
Memory (This wicked treasure!)
But
How weak it is!
While sliding on this mirror surface with ruffling waves
Seeking for the ring of a dream reflected
Chinese hieroglyphs hang on a woman's ample breast
Holding it for a moment
And being enveloped in flames
The falling object!

Yoshida

Atsumi Ikuko was born in 1940, and received a B.A. degree from Aoyama Gakuin University in 1964, and an M.A. in 1968. She completed a Creative Writing course at the University of British Columbia in 1964–65. She has been a lecturer at Aoyama Gakuin University since 1970 and has published two books of poetry, as well as translations, poems, and essays in several magazines.

Ayusawa Takako was born in Tokyo. She graduated from the International Christian University and is currently a teaching assistant in the Department of East Asian Languages and Literature at The University of Iowa.

John Bean was born in 1946, and received a B.A. degree in anthropology from Beloit College (Wisconsin), an M.A. in English and an M.F.A. in poetry from The University of Iowa. During the summers of 1969 and 1970, he received NDFL IV fellowships to study Japanese, and spent 1970–71 in Sendai, Japan, where he worked on a translation of Nishiwaki Junzaburo's *No Traveller Returns*. He has published poems and translations in several magazines, and was administrative assistant during 1973–74 for The University of Iowa's International Writing Program.

Gregory Campbell was born in Spokane, Washington, in 1938. He attended Eastern Washington College and the International Christian University in Tokyo. He has studied Zen in Japan.

Thomas Fitzsimmons is a poet and professor of English at Oakland University, Rochester, Michigan. He has published ten books of original poems, and has published *Japanese Poetry Now* (London: Andre Deutsch, 1972; New York: Schocken, 1973), a book of poems translated from the Japanese.

Fukuda Rikutaro is a professor at Tokyo University of Education, and has recently been a Fellow of the School of Letters at Indiana University. His publications include two books of original poems, and a number of books on American poetry.

David Goodman is presently in the Ph.D. program in Japanese literature at Stanford University. From 1969–73 he was editor of *Concerned Theatre Japan*, an English-language journal of the arts and society published in Tokyo as a part of Theatre Center 68, in which "Ballad of Soldiers" first appeared.

Ann Herring was born in Portland, Oregon. She studied classics, German literature, and later Japanese at the University of Washington. She is presently a full-time lecturer at Hosei University. She has published a translation of Japanese nursery rhymes called *Song of the Sour Plum* under the pen name of Hirawa Yasuko.

Inoue Kenji was born in 1929 and received a B.A. degree from Tokyo University in 1951. During 1959–60 he studied at Oberlin College, and is now a professor of English at Meiji University. His translations include books by William Faulkner, John Updike, Leslie Fiedler, J. D. Salinger, and LeRoi Jones.

Kijima Hajime was born in 1928 in Kyoto. He majored in

English literature at Tokyo University, and is currently a professor of English at Hosei University. He has published four books of poems, three novels, four books of essays, four books of short stories for children, and five picture books for children. In addition, he has edited two literary magazines: *New Japanese Literature* and *Twentieth Century Literature*, and has translated Walt Whitman, Langston Hughes, Nat Hentoff, and Julius Lester into Japanese. During 1972–73 he was a member of the International Writing Program at The University of Iowa.

Kobayashi Fukuko was born in Osaka in 1943. She received a B.A. degree in English from the University of North Carolina at Chapel Hill, and also a B.A. in English from the Osaka University of Foreign Studies. She received an M.A. from Waseda University and is teaching English there.

Takako Uchino Lento was born in Fukuoka, Japan. After receiving a B.A. and an M.A. from Japanese universities, she came to The University of Iowa as a Fulbright Fellow and earned an M.F.A. in creative writing. She has published translations and an article on modern Japanese poetry. In 1971 she published *The World Without Words*, a selection of Tamura Ryuichi's poetry in translation, under the auspices of the International Writing Program at The University of Iowa.

Nagatomo Shigenori was born in Kagoshima, Japan, in 1949, and was studying philosophy at The University of Iowa when engaged in translation.

J. Thomas Rimer was born in 1933, and received a B.A. degree in English literature from Princeton University in 1954, and an M.A. in Japanese literature in 1968 and a Ph.D. in Philosophy in 1971 at Columbia University. He is presently chairman of the Department of Chinese and Japanese at Washington University, St. Louis. He has published articles about Japanese literature, and several translations, and has two books soon to be published on modern Japanese theatre and on the historical stories of Mori Ogai.

Sato Hiroaki's translations from the Japanese have appeared in *Chelsea, Granite, Ironwood, Literature: East & West, MS., Telephone, WORKS,* and *The World.* Granite Publications has just published two collections of his translations, *Ten Japanese Poets,* and *Poems of Princess Shikishi,* and Chicago Review Press has published *Spring & Asura: Poems of Kenji Miyazawa. Chicago Review* published his "Anthology of Modern Japanese Poets" in a special Fall 1973 issue.

Whang Insu was born in Korea in 1928 where he lived until coming to Japan in 1936. He graduated from Tokyo University in 1951, majoring in English and American Language. Until 1968 he was a member of the General Association of Korean Residents in Japan, an organization working for a unified Korea. Presently he is an instructor at Hosei University in Tokyo.

Harold Wright was born in 1931 in Dayton, Ohio. After being stationed in Japan for several years with the U.S. Navy, he left the service to major in Japanese language and literature at the University of Hawaii. He did graduate work at Hawaii, Columbia University, and Keio University in Tokyo. Always interested in modern poetry, he has translated many of the modern Japanese poets. Forthcoming books include *Twentieth Century*

Japanese Poets and *Poetry of Tanikawa Shuntaro*. He currently teaches at Antioch College, Yellow Springs, Ohio, and spent the summer of 1973 in Japan where he videotaped modern Japanese writers for the Great Lakes College Association.

Yamada Yoshinari was born in 1927, graduated from Tokyo University of Education, and is presently an assistant professor of English at Iwate University, Morioka City, in northern Honshu.

Yamazaki Tsutomu was born in 1927 in Fukui Prefecture in Japan. He received a B.A. degree from Tokyo University and is now an assistant professor of English Literature at Senshu University, Tokyo. He has published translations of modern novels and articles, including Doris Lessing's *The Grass is Singing* and F. R. Benson's *Writers in Arms*.

Yoshida Yuriko was born in 1941. She graduated from Aoyama Gakuin University in 1964. She has studied the works of Lytton Strachey, and is now living in Tokyo.

INDEX